GENERATION EXPERIENCE

8 STEPS FOR
MATURE-AGE BUSINESS
SUCCESS

BONUS
"ARE YOU
READY?"
STEP

HUNTER LEONARD

Published by Silver & Wise Pty Ltd 2018
Silver & Wise Pty Ltd
PO Box 194, Bentleigh, VIC 3204
www.silverandwise.org.au

Copyright © Hunter Leonard

All rights reserved. Apart from any fair dealing for the purposes of study, research or review, as permitted under Australian Copyright Law, no part of this publication may be reproduced by any means without the written permission of the copyright owner. Every effort has been made to obtain permissions relating to information reproduced in this publication.

The information in this publication is based upon the current state of commercial and industry practice, applicable legislation, general law, and the general circumstances at the time of publication. No person shall rely on any of the contents of this publication and the publisher and the author expressly exclude all liability for direct and indirect loss suffered by any person resulting in any way from the use of or reliance on this publication or any part of it. Any opinions and advice are offered solely in pursuance of the author and publisher's intention to provide information, and have not been specifically sought.

National Library of Australia Cataloguing-in-Publication entry
Author: Leonard, Hunter
Title: Generation Experience: 8 steps for mature-age business success
Bibliography
Subjects: Business ownership

Dewey number: 658.0

Editor: Penny Springthorpe
Formatting services by BookCoverCafe.com

First edition 2018

ISBN 978-0992-298-746

Praise

"I have known Hunter for nearly ten years. We first worked together on the Council of the Australian Marketing Institute in Victoria. Hunter held a number of positions on the Council and was at one time the President of the Victorian Chapter of the AMI. Hunter is an outstanding marketing professional. He has a wealth of knowledge across a vast range of industries and business sectors. I have called upon on his expertise many times and always found him to be very helpful, creative and insightful when considering the development of a marketing strategy or trying to deal with a complex business marketing problem. I love discussing marketing problems with Hunter, because he always brings a surprise to the discussion in the form of a new of a new angle or direction others haven't considered. This is what makes Hunter special in the marketing community. At the next opportunity, I recommend that you meet Hunter, I would be happy to introduce you - just ask me."

John Thompson
Senior Manager, Road Safety Policy & Marketing–
Transport Accident Commission

"Hunter is a true marketing professional. Hunter has broad ranging skill sets and knowledge which can greatly assist an organisations marketing needs. He scopes marketing problems in detail and takes time to think deeply about strategic marketing options. Hunter's style engenders trust and he is great to work with."

Michael Dawson
General Manager, Marketing – Bluescope Steel

"Melbourne Brick & I engaged Hunter & BlueFrog Marketing back in 2004... where has 13 years gone!! It has been a fantastic partnership & that's exactly what having Hunter & his team engaged is like - it is a partnership & one we are very thankful for & don't take for granted. Hunter & his team understand the business's they are working with and even after 12 years we are still learning from the past & trying new initiatives & responding to the changes and challenges around us without losing focus on our core business ethos. We are looking forward to "cooking up a storm" with Hunter & his team for many more years to come as we continue on our business journey."

Matt Curtain
Managing Director, Melbourne Brick Group

"I publicised Hunter and his Rapid Marketing book to Australian media in 2010. What impresses me most is his ability to talk about marketing in a language everyone understands – he's jargon free. He makes marketing mainstream and media responded very well to him. One leading business journalist was so impressed after interviewing him, she attended his event – and ended up writing two articles. Hunter is very generous with his knowledge and able to apply it to a huge variety of businesses."

Katie McMurray
Katie Mac Publicity

"We first briefed Hunter in early 2010 to implement a formalised, measurable and strategic marketing platform into our organisation. Our expectations were very high and it is no overstatement to say they have been utterly exceeded!

Using a combination of smart technology overlaid with a thorough understanding of our business strategy and also process, Hunter has been instrumental in assisting us to embed key marketing concepts into the minds of our contracted sales force together with an active embracing of the processes necessary to grow the business.

We remain impressed with the dedication of Hunter and his team and look forward to our continued business association. I have no hesitation in recommending Hunter Leonard."

Adrian Kitchin
Managing Director of Resilium Insurance Broking

"Hunter is a consummate professional who is highly adaptable to various market sectors, he intently listens to your desired marketing outcomes and then delivers. It has been a pleasure knowing Hunter and his refreshing outlook that also entwines a community and social spirit."

Damian Seabrook
Altus Traffic

"Your Silver & Wise program is brilliant"
Lindsay Gordon
New Zealand Trade & Enterprise

"This initiative is not just about Hunter, he is on a mission to help hundreds, if not thousands of experienced business people who are over 40 and looking to run their own businesses. This will have a positive impact on their lives as well as adding a significant amount to the economy."

Jules Brooke
Handle your own PR

"I have a huge amount of respect for Hunter Leonard. He is certainly a visionary in the space of mature entrepreneurialism. In the coming years, as this market grows, Hunter will be leading the way, offering incredibly smart and strategic advice. My advice is to 'watch this space'. Congratulations Hunter."

Andrew Griffiths

Australia's #1 Small Business and Entrepreneurial Author and Speaker

Contents

Praise	iii
Foreword	xi
Preface	xiii
Introduction	xvi

STEP 0 ARE YOU BUSINESS READY? — xxi

1 Self-assessment	1
2 Is Business Ownership for You?	11
3 Before You Start	15
4 Who is Your Target Audience?	23
5 The Market Opportunity	26
6 The Basics of Starting and Running a Business	29
7 Equipment and other Resources	32
8 Technology	34
9 Your Role as Business Owner	38
10 Mind, Body and Spirit	40
11 Protect Yourself and Your Business	42

STEP 1 STRATEGY AND LEADERSHIP — 45

12 Your Business Model and Route to Market	47
13 Your Business Plan	50

STEP 2 MANAGING MONEY	**55**
14 Financing Your Business	57
15 Money In	62
16 Money Out	64
17 Recording and Reporting	66
STEP 3 MANAGING PEOPLE	**71**
18 Business Partners and Enablers	73
19 Suppliers	75
20 Hiring, Managing and Exiting Staff	77
STEP 4 MARKETING AND PUBLIC RELATIONS	**95**
21 The Importance of Value	97
22 The Seven Principles of Successful Marketing Organisations	101
23 Being a Good Corporate Citizen	113
24 Getting Customers to Talk About You	116
25 Getting the Media to Talk About You	118
STEP 5 SALES AND BUSINESS DEVELOPMENT	**123**
26 Your Target Audience	125
27 Steps in the Sales Process	128
28 Advocating for the Customer	138
STEP 6 DELIVERING ON PROMISES	**145**
29 Producing Your Product or Service	147
30 Delivering Products and Services	153
STEP 7 MANAGING QUALITY	**161**
31 Quality Management	163

STEP 8 FACING THE FUTURE — 173
    32 Adapt or Die — 175
    33 What Does Success Look Like? — 181
    34 What Is Your Exit Plan? — 183

    About Silver & Wise — 189
    About the Author — 192

Foreword

As the Australian Age Discrimination Commissioner, one of my responsibilities is to promote positive attitudes towards older Australians, and to combat ageism in all its forms, including discrimination in the workplace and job-selection process.

Ageism has resulted in many thousands of older Australians finding it difficult, if not impossible, to find employment. Certainly, there is an individual responsibility to maintain skills and be confident when searching for a role, but endemic discrimination is presenting a barrier to mature-age workers seeking employment.

While there are many companies that support mature-age workers, there is no doubt that others do not.

Although I raise awareness in my role as age-discrimination commissioner, we need organisations like Silver & Wise, and individuals like Hunter Leonard, who take the viewpoint that a solution is possible, and in Hunter's case that solution is helping mature-age individuals start their first business in their forties and beyond.

I can certainly see only positive outcomes from a program like this and encourage you to read this book closely to understand the methods Hunter is suggesting.

There is no doubt that increased productivity and the ability to remain an active part of society, right through to a point where individuals make their own choice over when to retire, has positive financial, social, physical and emotional impact. There are also broader implications for our entire economy.

I commend this book to you, as I do the many individuals like Hunter, who are leading the charge to make a difference to the lives of older Australians who are seeking to continue to contribute to our community and our economy, and their own wellbeing through paid work.

Kay Patterson

HON DR KAY PATTERSON AO
Age Discrimination Commissioner
October 2017

Preface

At the time of writing, I am a mature-age Aussie running two different organisations in business strategy and marketing: Blue Frog Marketing (founded in 2001), and Silver & Wise (founded in 2016). I work with business owners around the country, advising on marketing, value propositions and strategies, and I absolutely love what I do each day. I am passionate about working with business owners and marketing, which is how this book about mature-age business ownership came to be.

I was born in Canberra, ACT, where my father ran a business called ACT Floorcoverings with one of his mates. Just after my sister was born, my family moved to Baulkham Hills in Sydney. Dad worked in various jobs, but always came back to his own business, eventually running another business called Aranda Flooring (named after the Canberra suburb we lived in).

I distinctly remember going to work with Dad and helping, first with clean-up and later learning all the skills needed to lay vinyl and cork flooring; I still love the smell of cork tiles. Dad worked hard, and I remember some jobs going on until late in the evening, with Dad waiting for varnish coats to dry.

At fourteen, I started part-time work in a supermarket pushing trolleys, and then worked for a small nursery in Castle Hill called Alexander McDonald. There I learned pride in my work from the owner, who was willing to do anything to make the nursery well presented, including sweeping the paths up to thirty metres either side of his entrance every morning.

I also learned how to sell. The owner had a small hand painted picture in his office with the quotation: 'Selling is like shaving—if you don't do it at least once a day, you're a bum.'

After studying at university, I worked in the corporate world for over a decade, nine years of which was for a large pharmaceutical company, where I learned skills in sales and marketing. I became a product manager at twenty-five, and at thirty-three was made general manager of a world-leading healthcare advertising agency.

At thirty-five, I had an opportunity to start my own business when my first client made me an offer that was too good to refuse. I've been running that business, Blue Frog Marketing, for over seventeen years. It's been a challenge, and incredibly tough at times. I've made many mistakes, but I've learned from them. The business has been profitable for sixteen of those seventeen years, and this is an achievement I'm incredibly proud of. I'm also proud of the business's multiple awards for marketing excellence, and the fact that we got to nearly twenty staff at one stage in our growth.

In my marketing business, the times I'm most proud of are when we found exactly the right solution for a client in terms of marketing strategy, and went on to achieve amazing results and growth for them. To see the smiles on the faces of prosperous clients and know we played a part in that success—that is gold for me.

Over the years, I've also developed close personal friendships with suppliers, staff and customers, and those partnerships are the glue that has held the business together when times have been tough. The business has dealt with good and bad staff, suppliers and customers over those sixteen years, and we haven't always delivered on what we've promised. But on balance I think we've made a difference.

Personally, I've learned a lot during these past seventeen years, and if I call on my experience over the close to four decades I've been working,

I can easily see where my passion, skills and experience lie. Add to that the many surveys, the presentations to over fifteen thousand business owners, and the IP we developed over the years in terms of business strategies, processes and tools.

I believe Silver & Wise will build on those successes and create a real legacy. My goal is to make a measurable difference to the lives of mature-age people who are starting their first businesses after the age of forty.

Introduction

Congratulations. You're thinking about starting a business and you're forty-plus. My purpose in writing this book is to help people like you, those who are starting their first business at or after the age of forty. I am passionate about business ownership, and I believe that business begins at forty. In fact, I believe forty is an *excellent* time of life to begin business ownership. There are many reasons why, and I'll cover them in depth in the coming chapters.

I've worked with many mature-age business owners in a variety of different industries, and if you're starting a business, or are contemplating starting a business at a mature age, I feel like I know you already, even if we haven't met. I've written this book as an introduction to the challenges that individuals face in creating a business idea, bringing it to fruition, and being successful.

How did you get to this point? Chances are you are one of the tens of thousands of Australians in the forty-plus age group who have been made redundant from their job in corporate Australia. Maybe you've been looking for a new job and are finding it tough. You may even be among the 27 per cent of mature-age job seekers who have been on the receiving end of blatant age discrimination.

Alternatively, you may have come to a decision on your own terms. Perhaps you've decided that the corporate or working life is no longer for you, and you want to branch out on your own in a business you can control. There may be other challenges in your life that have led you

INTRODUCTION

to the threshold of one of the most exciting opportunities in your life: owning and running your own business.

For some reason, Western cultures, including Australia, do not value maturity, experience and wisdom as highly as they should. In Australia in 2018, there are over a hundred thousand mature-age individuals looking for work. That figure is growing, and growing too fast.

In this age group, it can take someone up to twice as long as younger job seekers to find another job after losing the previous one: on average as long as two years. Mature-age individuals are often told they're not vibrant or energetic enough, or they're not keeping up with technology, or one of several other nonsensical reasons given to them by employers or recruiters. I have a well-developed sense of fair play, and I hate to see a waste of talent, skills or opportunity because of embedded discrimination or small mindedness.

It doesn't matter what you don't have. It doesn't matter what you can't do. It doesn't matter how old you are or what political views you hold. All that matters is what you *do* have, what you *can* do, and what you *can* contribute.

As a potential business owner, you are about to become one of the most valued members of society; someone who is willing to take a risk, not just for themselves, but also for their community and society; someone who is productive and delivers something that is needed by others; someone who employs other people; someone who pays taxes and contributes. As a business owner, you will be a productive and highly valued member of your community.

With regard to the challenges that mature-age people face in the corporate and recruitment world, a similar situation occurs in marketing. Marketing is incredibly competitive. Some market players are ignored, others are not given opportunities, and it's not always the best product that wins.

My advice to clients in this situation is often to change their strategy, create a niche for what they're offering, and focus on the games they can win. My advice to mature-age job seekers is similar. Change the game plan. Stop looking for a job and create one for yourself by starting your own business.

If you are over forty and have had a long career as an employee, this may seem daunting. About two minutes after making the decision to start your own business, you might have an immediate moment of panic. *How do I do that?*

I have written this book to show you how, and also to encourage you to take the plunge. I have seen many people in this age group start and run their own businesses, and I know from experience that people over forty are well equipped with the experience and wisdom to be successful.

Success is a very personal measure. It relates to the setting and achieving of goals. It relates to achieving milestones, to wins small and large. For one person, huge success might be to completely cover all the expenses of the family in terms of home, car and food, and having a little left over for some fun. For someone else, success might be employing lots of people and building a reputation for excellence in their industry.

I realised early on that if Silver & Wise was successful in helping a few hundred business owners, it could have an impact on those owners, and the economy, in an order of magnitude many times larger than the revenue of those businesses. Deloitte published a research paper suggesting that just five per cent of mature-age Australians looking for work placed back into productive employment could have a multi-billion dollar impact on the GDP of the economy. So imagine what helping a few mature-age people start productive and successful businesses would do.

Once you've made the decision to start your own business, you'll have many questions. How will you structure the business? Is your idea a good one? What are your chances of success? Who will your customers be?

INTRODUCTION

Where will you set up your business? You're probably also worried about the financial security, or lack of it, with regard to running a business versus being an employee.

Yes, there are risks, but for moment, just relax. Get a cup of coffee or tea and start reading. I don't promise that starting and running a business will be easy, because it won't. But I do promise to be your guide, and to cover the most important aspects of starting and running a business so you are as well informed as possible.

By the end of the book, I hope you're confident enough to have a crack at it. Confident that you can build your knowledge and skills further and indeed become a successful and prosperous business owner. It will take time, and there will be challenges along the way, but you can do it.

STEP 0
ARE YOU BUSINESS READY?

CHAPTER 1
Self-assessment

As a mature-age business owner, you are in a unique position: you're in your forties or even older and you're about to start a business. In this chapter we examine some of the unique opportunities you have as a mature-age business owner, and also some of the risks that anyone, including you, has to take into account when starting a business.

First I want to emphasise that starting and running a business successfully has nothing to do with age. Let's right now agree to abolish any barrier related to your age that might be a holdover from your recent experience as an employee or job seeker.

Any lack of respect shown to mature-age workers, or discrimination based on age, is not related to the age itself; it's a social choice, an artificial construct in the minds of individuals who can't see beyond a few wrinkles and maybe a little silver hair. Those who display age-related discrimination forget that mature-age people with experience have created some of the most amazing inventions and businesses ever seen on this planet. For example:

- Alexander Cumming took out the patent for the flush toilet when he was forty-four.
- William Addis invented the first mass-produced toothbrush when he was forty-six.
- Wilhelm Conrad Roentgen formally discovered x-rays when he was fifty.
- Stephanie Kwolek was forty-two when she invented Kevlar.
- Henry Ford made the Model T when he was forty-five.
- Josephine Cochrane invented the dishwasher when she was forty-seven.
- Julia Child wrote her first cookbook at the age of fifty.
- Laura Ingalls Wilder published *Little House on the Prairie* at age sixty-five.

Your greatest opportunity in starting a business in your forties or older involves *you*: your experience working for others, your life experience, and the barriers you've faced and overcome. All of these things that make you who you are have been helping prepare you for the challenge of opening your own business.

One of the first things you can do when considering opening a business is to make a list of all the skills and knowledge you have. Review and analyse this list to identify the things you like to do the most, and like to do the least, and match the results to a range of business ideas where those skills and passions could be employed.

You may love gardening. Maybe you have experience working with agricultural chemicals on farms. You could start a business helping people choose plants for their gardens.

You may have worked as a corporate finance manager, so you can certainly help business owners with their cash flow.

I guarantee that there are opportunities to create businesses in areas that suit your skills and your passions.

Never believe anyone who tells you that your skills are out-dated or being surpassed by technology. It isn't true, just as the original estimate for a worldwide market for computers at just six units—from a former IBM employee—wasn't true.

Sure, you might need to learn some new skills. You might have to work out how to use Xero for your accounts instead of keeping a shoebox full of receipts. But you've done it before and you can do it again. All you have to do is decide. When you run a business, you will always be learning new ways of doing things; that will never change.

Existing resources

Another opportunity you have when you start a business as a mature-age individual is to utilise any networks you have built up over the years. You've spent years working with people, and you probably have a large group of friends and colleagues. When you start your own business, this network will come in very handy for testing ideas, conducting surveys, and asking for referrals to friends and colleagues who might need your help.

Take a blank piece of paper and make a mind map of all the people you know. Collect them into specific groups; for instance, all the people you know who work in finance, or all the people you know who run their own business, or all the people you know working in PR, or all the people you know who live in your suburb.

Then review this list, and circle those who could potentially help you with your specific business idea, either by partnering with you, making referrals on your behalf, or using their professional help to serve your business.

Research tells us that people who start their business at a mature age generally have more money to invest. The figures for averages tell us that mature-age people tend to invest more in their business, and they are also more successful at generating higher profits than younger business owners. The reasons why these people are more successful than others are not totally clear, but their success could quite possibly be linked to experience, networks and resources. I think you can safely make that assumption about yourself, too.

Imagine a line charting a person's life by their age in years. The line would probably look like a hump. It would go up the scale until midlife and then head down towards the bottom after that. This is sometimes called a bell curve.

The problem is that corporations and recruiters seem to think that midlife hits, it's literally all downhill from there and so they get rid of people of this age. I prefer to see this curve as continuing upward, that in midlife we're all just getting started. That the momentum of productivity, earning potential and wisdom can keep going upwards.

Risks

Every business owner faces risks to their business. Running a business is by definition an uncertain and risky exercise. It used to be a lot more risky than being an employee, but as you may have noticed, there is no surety in being an employee anymore either. Being successful comes down to the simplicity of making the most of opportunities, and also being aware of and handling potential risks in business.

You may have heard the term 'SWOT analysis'. This is a management tool that helps prepare action plans that utilise strengths and weaknesses, and outlines the opportunities and threats in a particular business. A good business owner uses this tool well, and regularly.

Some time ago I took a personality and psychometric test called a Q-score. This is basically a review of how an individual sees opportunity and risk. It is a score that balances these two as a ratio. If you have a five-times score biased towards opportunity, you are five times more likely to see an opportunity versus acknowledging a risk.

I have a confession. I scored one of the highest ever ratios of opportunity versus risk. I'm what is known as an 'outlier', which means I'm on the extreme edge when it comes to seeing opportunities. I'm aware that this is a potential weakness, and so I surround myself with mentors and business partners who are better at analysing risk than I am. And I also make sure I'm very careful about assessing the risks in any situation. Otherwise I'm likely to chase opportunities hard without seeing the dangers.

You may be the same; you may be different. In the end it doesn't matter—as long as you're aware and put in place actions to cover your bases in your business.

Let's examine some of the risks that any business owner faces, a few of which are unique to mature-age individuals.

The first risk a business owner faces is not doing enough research about the opportunity they are chasing *before* they start the business. I've seen many examples of businesses that get a long way down the track to developing a new product or business, including spending thousands on product samples, or even leasing office space, before they've spoken to even one prospect or potential customer.

Be cautious. Learn as much about a business opportunity as possible before investing too much money (more about this later).

Competition is always a risk in business (more about this later as well). It's rare for anyone to start a business without at least one or two competitors in the immediate area. Regardless of whether it's garden maintenance, accounting or picture framing, someone else will be offering that service or product to the same target audience as you.

Being disconnected from your customers is another huge risk in business. Research shows that less than twenty per cent of businesses survey their customers regularly to find out their needs and wants. If you don't know what customers think of you, or what they need, it's going to be pretty difficult to develop good products and services.

And of course age is a factor. There's an inherent risk in starting a new business at a mature age. I realise that I've stated firmly that I don't care about age, and that it shouldn't make a difference. I do strongly believe that age shouldn't make a difference in terms of societal attitudes, but there are indisputable risks in being older and starting a business.

One is health. Running a business is not for the faint-hearted. You need to be energetic, active and healthy. At the very least, you should be eating well, getting enough sleep, and doing some exercise that is appropriate for you. I ride my bike regularly, try to eat nutritious foods, and definitely aim to get at least seven hours of sleep a night. If you're running a business, you will benefit from being fit, healthy and rested.

There's enough great data out there about this, so I'm not going to labour the point, and for sure I'm not an expert on exercise and eating. But I do advise you to make this a part of your daily, weekly and monthly routine.

Another risk you may want to consider is succession planning. Even though you're only just starting, or about to start, your business, you may only run it for five, ten or fifteen years. Best-practice advice always tells the business owner to have an exit strategy from the beginning. Even if you're starting a small consulting business, such as a gardening service, you might want to think about what you're going to do with the business when you decide to move on.

It doesn't matter what you decide. There are no right or wrong options, whether it's preparing the business for sale, or employing another person to run it, or simply closing it down. Choose what you think is right for you, and make a plan now. Even if you don't know how it will actually work out, at least set some goals on how you'd *like* it to work out. We tend to get what we aim for, so aim for what *you* want.

I've already discussed the attitude of corporate and recruitment agencies towards mature-age individuals. It's also possible that someone starting a business in their forties or fifties could experience some discrimination based on their age, and this is another risk factor. In every business there is an inherent risk relating to age.

Every business I've ever worked in has produced a product or service whose primary target was defined by age or sex. For example, I launched an osteoporosis product that was mainly targeted at women aged fifty and over who had low bone density. But I've also helped market products aimed mainly at men aged eighteen to thirty-five.

To minimise the risk of age-related issues in your business, take this factor into account with your choice of business opportunity. If your business is service related, find a target audience that will value your experience. If it's a product business, age will probably not be as big an issue because you won't be the face of the business.

There are other risks in running a business, some related to your skills, some related to the market, and some related to the team you build around you. These will all be covered later in the book, but for now just be aware that certain risks exist, and that you'll need to put in place actions to take care of them.

Competence

Most dictionaries define competence as having the necessary ability, knowledge, or skill to do something successfully. When you decide to become a business owner, you will need a range of common skills. By common, I mean skills that are universally required in any business.

Most business owners start a business because they love, or are good at, some specific technical skill. Maybe it's a specialty: hanging pictures, making violins, accounting, insurance. It's quite rare for someone to have what might be called 'general management' skills when they start a new business.

In our business, which uses benchmarks of over ten thousand business owners, we regularly see people challenged by issues such as managing money, people, cash flow, or time management. One of my favourite quotes is 'the role of the generalist is to foster communication among specialists'. I think I first heard that when I was doing a botany course at university and it has stuck with me throughout my whole life. As a business owner, you have to be a generalist with a wide range of skills.

If you start a new business in garden maintenance, for example, you will probably be pruning and fertilising plants, installing sprinklers, mowing lawns and so forth. You'll have to have these technical skills. But if you want to run a really successful business, you'll also have to have a series of general-management skills—and be competent in them, at least until your business is big enough to hand these specialist tasks off to an expert. And even then, your key responsibility as business owner will be to ensure that these specialised tasks are being done.

In the first year of running my first business, I focused heavily on my technical skills. I provided excellent marketing plans for my first clients and I helped them achieve some good growth in the sales of their products. But twelve months in, I got a big shock with the finances of our business when I received a fairly hefty tax bill. The problem was that I didn't have the skills or competence to know how to organise the accounts and tax. You can be assured that I rapidly learned that skill, and put in place policies and procedures to make sure it didn't happen again.

I've run into many challenges like this. On another occasion, the consultancy business had a bad debt of over $20,000 when clients refused to pay—and then one out of business themselves. Once again, I didn't have the competence to have policies in place to collect payments up front before doing the work. And once again, I quickly put in place procedures and policies to avoid this happening in the future.

My point is that I'm not talking about theory here. You *will* have to be competent in a range of business disciplines to run an effective business. And you *will* make mistakes. The aim of this book is to help you overcome or avoid these mistakes by sharing what I've learned. By covering the key areas, I hope you will be prepared for any eventuality.

Will you avoid all these issues? No, but hopefully you'll be better prepared.

As I've developed my knowledge and skills, and put in place policies and procedures in these areas, the running of the business has certainly become easier, and a lot more fun, too. I'm not a finance expert, and nor am I an expert in human resources. But I will share what I've learned, and will act as your guide and mentor regarding what you'll need to put in place in your business. Oh, and by the way, I've asked a lot of experts along the way about this, too.

In fact, we have a technical advisory board in Silver & Wise consisting of people who are specialists in their fields, who practise these skills daily in their own businesses, and who have been kind enough to share their specialist wisdom with me, so I can pass it on to you.

I'm performing the role of generalist fostering communication among specialists, and passing knowledge onto other generalists. The business owner: you.

Remember well the definition of competence: the ability, skill or knowledge to make a success of something.

Skills

There are eight key skills any business owner needs in order to be successful in running a business:

1. An understanding of business strategy and where value comes from
2. Competence in planning, implementing and measuring strategic marketing programs; building the public profile of a business through PR, and delivering on promises, which also contributes to value
3. An ability to convert any leads or prospects or to attract, develop and retain high-quality sales staff to perform this role
4. An ability to hire, develop and retain high-quality staff
5. An ability to manage money, including knowledge of profit-and-loss sheets, balance sheets, legislation and cash flow
6. An ability to produce and deliver valued and therefore profitable products and/or services to the target market of the business
7. An ability to understand what quality is, and how to manage it in a business that sells products, services or both
8. A willingness to be adaptable to changes in the market, competition, customers and their own business to continue to be successful over time

It's important to remember that while you may not need to be experienced or competent in each one of these things personally, you definitely need to ensure that they're being done. It is likely you will start your business as a sole trader and will do these things yourself. You might make some mistakes or need some training or get some guidance from your network until you can them over to your bookkeeper, sales person, marketing person or customer-service staff. These are non-negotiable activities that must be done to ensure the continued success of any business. These eight skills form the backbone of the rest of this book, and are indeed the 8 steps you need to start and run a successful business.

Chapter 2
Is Business Ownership for You?

You may have seen advertisements for purchasing franchises or other businesses showing a photo of someone sitting on the beach drinking a cocktail, enjoying all the freedom that running a business has given them. The idea is to compare this picture with being an employee trapped in some ogre's dungeon. I'm sure the people who put those ads together never ran their own business.

In this chapter, I'm not going to sugarcoat what running a business really means. It can be tough, something that employees will never understand. It can be a life of insecurity. There will be days when you feel a deep pit in your stomach, wondering how you're going to solve a particular issue, knowing that there's no one except you to take responsibility for it.

But running a business can also be joyous and exciting in a dancing-around-the room-like-an-idiot king of way when one of your plans comes off, and you know that *you're* the one who made it happen.

So let's get on with it: the good, the bad and the ugly.

The good

There are many great things about running a business, provided you run it well and take care to do all the things you need to do to shepherd your 'baby' along. Being the boss is pretty cool. When you start a business, you're chief cook and bottle washer, but you're also in control of your own destiny, and that can be an awesome feeling.

I remember the first day I sat down at my desk in my home office—a nook at one end of the dining room—and made my first phone call as a business owner. On my second-hand desk were a computer, a phone, and some stationery. It was exciting. As was the first day I received payment from my first client; I still have the photo of me holding the cheque.

I've changed business strategies several times over the past sixteen years, going from a sole trader set-up to a small number of staff, then buying a complementary-product business from a mate, then starting a second business division, and then tearing up the playbook, outsourcing everything and going back to being sole employee again.

Each time I made a change, I was only able to do so because I was in control. I decided and I made the changes—with a little sage advice from my wife and business partner to head me in the right direction.

Our business has won awards for our marketing work, and being able to accept those awards and share some of our journey with my industry peers has been awesome. It's definitely sweeter when it's your own business.

The bad

Being the boss can also be difficult at times. When I've had to counsel a staff member who wasn't doing the right thing. When I've had to exit a staff member who wasn't performing.

At times I've felt sick in the stomach when the cash flow was really tight, and I wasn't sure how I was going to pay the bills or pay the staff on time. I've had many sleepless nights, where I've woken up with my mind spinning, trying to find a solution for an issue with a staff member, client or supplier.

When you begin running your own business, you will have times like this, too. If you're well skilled and organised in the way you operate, you'll minimise the number of times these things happen, but they will still happen. At times a business seems like an eel: the harder you try to hold onto it, the slipperier it becomes.

It can be tough at times to switch off and get away, because clients are always relying on you to get things done. And turning out the light and heading overseas for a three-week holiday in Europe just doesn't work when you run your own business.

The ugly

The ugly side of running a business will happen, too. I can offer three examples of this from my sixteen years.

The worst was when a client didn't pay a $20,000 bill, which absolutely devastated the cash flow for nearly a year. It cost another $10,000 in legal fees to chase it and we still didn't get paid. After that, you can be sure we put in place policies about up-front payment for services.

Another terrible time was when my family and I went to Bali for a fortieth birthday. I picked up an Aussie paper and saw a full-page advertisement about a massive recall of products. One of our two major clients was caught up in it, and I realised that overnight we had lost fifty per cent of our revenue. The rest of the holiday wasn't that much fun.

One of the worst situations I experienced was finding out that a key staff member was operating unethically during their time with us. They were moonlighting for one of our client's major competitors at nighttime. It was a terrible situation, and we risked losing a key client. I felt genuinely sick and betrayed, and needless to say we terminated the person on the spot. Given our key relationship, I had to then share the information with our client. Luckily they trusted me and were willing to leave any action at that, but they were not happy.

We had invested a lot in this individual, who, fortunately, was not a senior team member. Almost all of our key staff—general managers, client service directors, account directors—have been talented and high-quality employees, some of whom have even become good friends over the years.

As a business owner, you will almost certainty encounter ugly problems like this. It may not be cash flow or bad debt, but it could be product recalls, customer complaints, or theft.

I did say that I wasn't going to sugarcoat it. I've had many discussions with friends and clients, and I can tell you that they have all experienced the good, bad and ugly of business ownership. They've employed the wrong people, they've had products recalled, they've lost tens of thousands in stock, and they've had their computers shut down in ransom ware attacks.

But despite the downsides of owning a business, I would never want to work for someone else again. I love owning a business. I love working with business owners. They are some of the most driven, passionate and courageous people I know. Many do amazingly philanthropic things with a share of their profits. And many take risks to enjoy the rewards of business ownership that an employee would never understand.

So, all power to the business owner. It's a pretty awesome thing to be.

After reading this chapter, you might have decided that running a business isn't for you. That's perfectly okay. You might decide to start looking for another way to make money. Whatever you choose to do, do it well. But if you're on-board for the ride, strap in and let's get into it.

Chapter 3
Before You Start

Now that we've got the preliminary work out of the way—especially the good, bad and ugly of being a business owner—it's time to introduce a simple tool called the 'business readiness scorecard'. It's a set of simple questions that you can answer right now. Accompanying each question is a brief explanation of the reasons for asking it. When you've read this, I suggest you immediately benchmark yourself before going onto the next question.

1. Are you passionate about the idea of starting your own business? Passion is an incredibly important factor in starting a business. Running a business can be hard at times, but if you have passion you'll be able to take the hits and overcome any barriers you encounter. You'll be willing to do what it takes to realise your goals and dreams. To be successful, you have to have passion, and you have to back yourself.
2. Do you have something you are good at? Putting ego and confidence aside for a moment, if you're going to start a business you have to have some 'game', as it's sometimes called. Before you have a

business name, a nice logo, or fancy websites and brochures, your business and its value will rely on you and your own reputation.

When I started my first business in marketing consulting, I already had nearly fifteen years of experience in sales and marketing. I also knew many people who were aware of what I could do and they backed me when I went out on my own. I don't believe in the fake-it-until-you-make-it mantra that some people profess to follow. I believe that you start with a skill, and then build a business around that.

3. Would you be passionate about running a business around this skill? Now we're back to passion again, but with a different perspective. Imagine you had studied accounting and worked in an accounting function in a large corporate for many years. It might seem logical to take that skill and go out on your own in your own accounting practice. But what if you couldn't stand the thought of looking at another set of books? What if it gave you chills just contemplating it? In that case, my advice would be not to do it.

Financial skills can be applied in many different ways. In this situation, you could be better off starting another business where your accounting skills could be applied, but not in the traditional compliance model of accounting. It could be focused on helping businesses sort out their cash flow or financing, or helping start-ups work out their business model for investors.

Or you could decide to use your financial knowledge as the basis of a product or service business. In this case, you would be ahead of many other business owners due to your ability to work the numbers.

4. Do you believe that the world—or at least your market—needs your skill? You will find this out later in your business planning and research of the market, but for now a quick answer is all that's needed. Do you believe there is a market? Belief is an important part of being

CHAPTER 3: BEFORE YOU START

confident enough to take the leap. That answer is all that's needed in a readiness score for now.

5. Could you get paid for this skill? Once again, the nitty-gritty can be worked out later. But if you know of people who are being paying for doing this skill that you possess, then the answer is yes. Thirty years ago, if you had said that you wanted to start an online-shopping business for consumers you wouldn't have been able to do it. The skills, or channel, didn't exist. But with the advent of the Internet, and shopping giants like Amazon and eBay, many new skills and roles have been created.

   Every skill needs a market willing to pay for it, so make sure you can answer yes to this question. An interesting example of this is the recent explosion in RTO training courses. It's clear that some businesses in these markets were creating too big a supply of certain occupations, like massage therapy, for instance, without an eye on the overall market demand for these. Consequently, the cost of massages has dropped markedly in recent years, and there is an oversupply of massage therapists in the market as a result. Years ago, guilds and associations put in place high entry barriers to manage supply and demand, but these barriers have been removed and the market has been damaged as a result.

6. Are you willing to learn other skills you'll need to run this business? Take it from me, you will never run a successful business based purely on the specialist technical skills you used as an employee. An organisation is a very different beast to a single job. There are at least eight specific skill competencies that a good business owner will need.

   Larger organisations can compartmentalise these with specialist experts in each area, but the small-business owner, for a while at least, does have to be a generalist and know how to do the basics of many roles, everything from strategy to customer service, finance to HR, marketer to salesperson.

Even with cheaper global task-based outsourcing, a small business often doesn't have the volume, margin or revenue to afford the outsourcing of specialist skills, which means that until it does, you're the person responsible.

7   Do you like dealing with people? Even with the proliferation of online businesses, and the use of technology to replace personal interaction in stages of manufacture, supply, production, selling and distribution, as a business owner you will have to deal with people at some stage—your accountant, business partners, staff, customers, suppliers.

This is an important point, and one you need to consider to avoid problems down the road. Think of a corporate manager, for instance, getting a redundancy payment and buying a cafe or franchise business, when deep down they actually prefer to be in an office cubicle cranking out a product or service. If you don't like the thought of dealing with, managing, leading or inspiring people, or selling to customers, then owning a business is probably not for you.

8   Do you have enough financial reserves to last at least six months without making money from your business? Despite the miracle overnight-success stories reported on social media, and the belief that it's easy to become a millionaire now that we're dealing in the global economy, most of these tales are fantasy. Every business has a start-up phase, and it often takes quite a while for a new business to generate *any* revenue, let alone enough to cover expenses and pay the owner.

Some might say that if it doesn't work fast it isn't a good business in the first place, but you will have to get a good grip on the things that have to happen in order to start your business and get it rolling.

First, you have to develop the product or service. Then you have to set up and structure the business. Then you have to start communicating to a target audience what you are offering. Then they have to become aware of that fact. It takes time for people to consider what's on offer and change their patterns of behaviour. Then there are competitors to consider. Finally, some customers might eventuate.

All of this might be quick or it might be slow, but if you haven't got some financial backing for a minimum amount of time, you're taking a bigger risk than is necessary in starting your business.

I was fortunate when starting my first business. I had a signed offer from a client before I began, which covered my start-up phase and funded my first six months. But in my new business, I developed products and services for twelve to eighteen months before I saw the first invoice go out and get paid. That was over $250,000 in time and resources invested before I received the first piece of revenue.

Every business is different, but make sure you have at least some backing for a minimum time. Six months is the minimum. How you fund this will depend on your personal circumstances. It could be your own money, or a client's or the bank's. Just ensure that you're covered.

9   Do you have a good personal network of prospects that might buy from you if you started a business? Many businesses rely on the personal productivity of the owner when starting, and what better place to start than your own network that you've built up over many years? Research it before you start, and convert prospects from your network when you do. It might be the most important part of your new business.

10 Do you have a business idea in mind already? It can take time to come up with a business idea, so if you have one already that's a very good start.

Your readiness scorecard

Now that you've read through the questions, and the explanations behind them, use the following table to score yourself on your readiness. Do this right now, without delay. You can always come back and redo the scorecard at any time.

Question	Circle Yes/No
Are you passionate about the idea of starting your own business?	Yes/No
Do you have something you are good at?	Yes/No
Would you be passionate about running a business around this skill?	Yes/No
Do you believe that the world (or at least your market) needs your skill?	Yes/No
Could you get paid for this skill?	Yes/No
Are you willing to learn other skills you'll need to run this business?	Yes/No
Do you like dealing with people?	Yes/No
Do you have enough cash or finance to last at least six months without making money or pay from your business?	Yes/No

If you scored 6 or less, you're probably not ready yet, so focus on each *no* in your list and turn it into a *yes*.

If you scored 7 or 8, you could probably consider getting going straightaway. As you prepare to start your business, you can work on the last couple of *no* answers and turn them into *yes*.

If you scored 9 or 10, what are you waiting for? You should have started already.

Benchmarking for the business owner

This is a book about generalist skills that every business owner needs. If you notice a specific gap in your skills, pay particular attention to the chapter that covers that skill area. You may not need the skill from day one, but at some stage you will need it, or at the very least you will need the systems and processes to ensure that the skill is covered in your organisation.

Just being aware that a skill or competency is needed is a good start.

If you're already an expert in marketing, or finance or HR or quality management, you might find those chapters unnecessary. Obviously, the vast breadth of running a business can't be covered in one book. It's not possible to get into the finer details of conflict resolution in handling people, or the local legislation with regard to hiring and firing staff in every state or country where this book is read. You can probably skim over those chapters to keep the thread of the book going.

Make a note of the chapters you want to skim (due to pre-existing skills) or pay close attention to (due to a skill or knowledge gap). Enjoy the process and then move onto the next chapter in your business start-up journey.

1. Rate your skills in strategic planning out of 10.
2. Rate your skills in leadership out of 10.
3. Rate your skills in managing money out of 10.
4. Rate your skills in managing people out of 10.
5. Rate your skills in quality management out of 10.
6. Rate your skills in sales and business development out of 10.
7. Rate your skills in your specific product or service out of 10 (e.g. you can make violins and want to run a violin-making business).
8. Rate your skills in client service out of 10.
9. Rate your skills in marketing and PR out of 10.
10. Rate your skills in time management out of 10.

If you rated yourself a 6 or less on any question, you should definitely focus on that section of the book.

If you scored 7 or 8 out of 10, you will still learn something from that chapter.

If you scored 9 or 10 out of 10, you probably find yourself nodding regularly through that chapter and are familiar with the key skills you need in that part of your business.

If your total score was less than 40 out of 100, we advise you to consider coming to one of our introductory workshops in order to explore whether business ownership is right for you, and definitely look at this carefully before you go out and start your own business or buy one.

Chapter 4
Who is Your Target Audience?

I recently interviewed my good mate, Tim Reid, founder of Australia's number one marketing podcast: *Small Business, Big Marketing*. We talked about marketing a small business and he told me that whenever he presents or writes about his business, he always has 'Daz' in mind. Daz is Tim's ideal customer, someone who represents all the qualities of the ideal person he wants to do business with. Who is your Daz?

Understanding your target audience goes beyond their age, location, and how much income they have. It means understanding what they need and want in relation to your product and service. You need to understand what is important to them, how they purchase that product and service, what media they consume, and what motivates them. To identify and understand a target audience, you need to research them.

In our benchmarks at Blue Frog Marketing, we find that over eighty-five per cent of businesses have *not* conducted research into their customers in the previous twelve months.

Basing business operations on assumptions about who buys the product or service, and what they need and want, is a dangerous game to play. And like our wise owl on the front cover, you should never base starting a business on an assumption.

What do your customers think of your business idea?

Beyond your product and service, there is the business model you are selecting to go to market.

A business model is defined as a plan for the successful operation of a business, identification of sources of revenue, and researching the intended customer base, products, and details of financing.

Where is your revenue coming from in your business? How many customers will it take to get to your revenue targets? How are you financing the business?

There are many questions to be asked in this area, and it's wise to ask and answer these questions before investing too much time in actually developing product or services. Value is an important theme we'll come back to again in this book.

A customer will place a certain value on your product or service, and that value will have to be equal to and preferably higher than the price in order for them to purchase it or they could value service or follow up or reliability. They will be doing these calculations, even if these are subconscious, about how your product or service compares to other options they have. We'll get into value in detail later on, but for now, understand that you have to deliver value in order to build a business.

Who is the competition and how good are they?

There is virtually no market today that has no competition. It's rare for any business to have an exclusive market. In order to run a successful business, you need to understand how you compare to the competition around you in your market.

What do they do well or poorly in comparison to you? What are some of the problems or concerns the customers of existing competitors have that might offer an opening to you? What do your competitors do well that you'll have to at least match for customers to buy from you (e.g. fast delivery)?

Making a decision

Before you get full steam into developing your business product or service, this chapter should have provided answers to the questions you need to be asking. You should now be well informed enough to be able to make the hard decisions about whether you're ready to launch, or whether to go back to the drawing board with a better or different idea for your business.

Go into the process with your eyes wide open to the opportunities *and* the challenges, and you'll be well on the way to success when you do launch.

Chapter 5
The Market Opportunity

You *must* research any idea you have for a business to determine its potential for success in the location you want to operate in. I've seen many examples of individuals who think they have a million-dollar idea and go about setting up the business, finding premises, developing product and so forth, all based on their own assumptions about the idea or business.

The ramifications of making assumptions and investing money in an unproven idea are serious. They can include wasting a huge amount of money, time and energy, and can also lead to an early and costly closure of the business.

While your passion for a business is important, its commercial success will not be related to how good you think it is. Success rests on two questions: Do customers need or want the idea? Will you be able to compete effectively with other businesses in that market at a price level that allows you to make a profit?

Research is one of the first things to do if you're starting a new business, even if you're simply purchasing an existing one. Find out what customers need and want. Then organise your business around that and you're far more likely to be successful than someone who hasn't done the research.

Second in importance to research is knowing you can also price the product or service at a level in your target area that allows you to make a profit. Here is a checklist of how to go about assessing a market opportunity for a business idea:

1. Decide on the territory you want to operate in. Start-up businesses usually begin in a local suburb or region before they expand on a state or national basis. You might never expand your operations beyond the local suburb. Just be aware of the territory.
2. Research all the other businesses (competition) in the area that offer the same service as you. If you can, find out exactly what they offer, how much they charge, whom they are targeting in terms of customers, and what people think of them.
3. Decide on your target audience: male, female, age, income levels, and other demographics.
4. Find out how much of your target audience lives or works in the territory you want to operate in. For example, if you're targeting farmers in a particular area, you'd like to know that there are a hundred or a thousand of them, and how this might relate to the opportunity in terms of income and revenue you could expect if you got, say, one per cent of the total available market. Would that be a reasonable assumption? Or would you struggle to meet your goals even if you got one hundred per cent? (An unlikely scenario in any market.)
5. Select a few people from your target audience and survey them on your product or service idea. Find out what they think, what concerns them, how much they pay now for that service, what they think about their current choices, and how likely they would be to switch to

your offering. All this data is useful in defining the potential of your product. Too many businesses open up in a particular area and spend money on fit-outs and development without checking to see if there's a real opportunity.

6   Based on your research, calculate the potential of your business. Be realistic about how many clients you can get and how tough the competition will be. How much revenue do you need to make to break even? How much to make a profit? And how many customers will each outcome require? Take your time and be conservative.

Chapter 6
The Basics of Starting and Running a Business

Before we get into discussing the skill areas you need to be confident in, it's important to discuss the basics of starting and running a business. These include registering your business, getting a name, possibly finding a domain (web address) that matches your name, and registering a trademark if you want to.

You need to communicate with organisations like the Australian Tax Office or inland-revenue department, and be registered for GST. You need to decide on the structure of your business. Will you operate it as a sole trader, a joint venture, a company, or a trust? There are the issues of hiring people and employment legislation. You may need to get insurance, including work cover. There are numerous helpful resources on national and state government websites for all of these issues.

As you learn the skills necessary to become a business owner, make sure you take care of the absolute basics of registration, law and tax.

Structure of your business

There are numerous ways to structure a business. The most common ways are sole trader, partnership, proprietary limited company, and trust, but these will differ depending on the state or country.

All business structures are designed with two purposes in mind: the liability of the operators, and how the business should be treated for tax purposes. Without getting technical about it, these are the main reasons why you want to structure your business in an appropriate way for your own situation. It's not my role to recommend structures, but rather to recommend that you look at your options carefully with an expert. In this way, you will be less likely to get into problems where you have the wrong structure, your assets aren't protected, or your tax situation isn't suitable to your personal requirements.

Naming your business

While there is legislation and a process associated with registering a business name, and protection afforded to a unique business name, the process of naming a business is something you can do, and it can be creative and fun.

At Silver & Wise, we used a directed brainstorm approach to come up with a name, and we've also named a lot of other businesses, products and services as well. Have fun with the process. If you want your business name to stand out, enjoy the process of coming up with something that is relevant and also engages your potential clients.

Some of my favourite names have a relevance to the product or service, *and* a sense of humour. For instance, I like the way Thai restaurants often come up with names that play on the word 'Thai', e.g. Bow Thai.

CHAPTER 6: THE BASICS OF STARTING AND RUNNING A BUSINESS

The directed brainstorming process:

1. Consider the different categories of names, e.g. symbolic (Shell), technical (WD-40), service or benefit related (Assure Insurance), scientific (Panadol), or made up from another source (Adidas).
2. Pick a category, and then brainstorm within that category for five to ten minutes with a group of staff or friends using a whiteboard or flipchart.
3. Once you've brainstormed one category, pick another and repeat.
4. Once you've brainstormed all categories, give the participants three to five stickers and ask them to vote for their favourites.
5. Add up all the votes and select the top three to five names most voted for.
6. Check the favourite names against existing business names and trademarks.

With respect to business names and trademarks, its important to know that registering a business name does not necessarily give you protection over that name. You will need to seek advice if you want to make sure your favourite name is both available and protectable. Once you've determined whether you can get your chosen website or domain name, it's important to check social-media pages and other Internet forums.

Beyond naming a business, you'll also want to start considering your logo and brand. There are whole processes associated with writing a brief for a web designer, who will build a range of image and marketing collateral for your business. But don't do any of that before you check the basics.

Is the name available? Can you protect it? Is anyone else operating with a similar name in the same market? And so on. Have fun.

Chapter 7
Equipment and other Resources

Every business needs equipment and other resources in order to operate. Only buy equipment as and when you need it, and don't overdo it too early. You risk tying up too much of your capital and resources if you over-engineer things.

When we first started our business Blue Frog Marketing, we had a black-and-white printer, a computer, a fax machine and a second-hand desk from the local furniture wholesaler. We added a large colour printer to the office after a few years, but if we needed colour printing done on an ad-hoc basis, I would drop into Officeworks. That was better than having the expense of running a full-colour printer in our office. We had instant coffee and teabags in our office kitchen, and eventually we purchased a pod coffee machine.

If you're in a service business, you can probably operate from home initially rather than signing up for an expensive lease on an office. Or you could go into an innovation hub or co-working space.

CHAPTER 7: EQUIPMENT AND OTHER RESOURCES

A product business might be different. You may have to buy equipment to produce things, but again, do it on a gradient. Until you establish your business, attract regular customers and begin to grow, you don't want to overinvest, overcommit or overcapitalise.

Here is a checklist:

- What equipment do you need?
- Can you access it from someone else temporarily?
- Can you get it second-hand?
- Do you really need the high-end model, or can you use the basic one to start with?
- If you do need equipment, when do you need it? Can you get it just before you need it?
- If in doubt, don't buy and don't commit.

Chapter 8
Technology

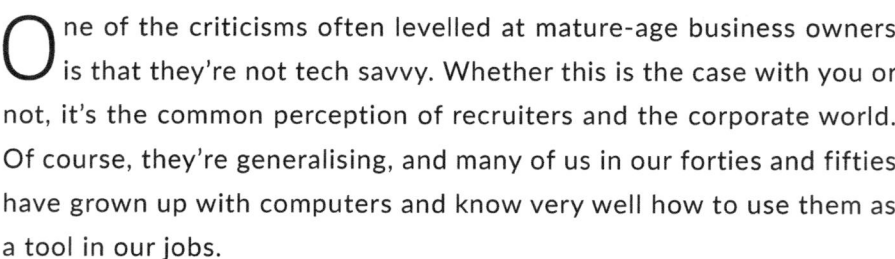

One of the criticisms often levelled at mature-age business owners is that they're not tech savvy. Whether this is the case with you or not, it's the common perception of recruiters and the corporate world. Of course, they're generalising, and many of us in our forties and fifties have grown up with computers and know very well how to use them as a tool in our jobs.

Be that as it may, when you start a business in your forties and fifties you're probably going to be exposed to more technology that you have been in, say, a specialist corporate role.

There are five key pieces of technology you will not want to live without in your business. And despite what corporates and recruiters say, you'll find them easy to use, cost effective and accessible, no matter what your age, or experience with technology in the past. Enjoy the benefits of using them in your business.

Cloud bookkeeping

This has absolutely revolutionised my world in the past five years. I've been running businesses for sixteen years, and from day one had MYOB on my computer. Despite this software being 'technology', it was a relatively dumb filing system for financial records. Sure, it was a step up from the shoebox, but it didn't communicate with the bank, accountant etc.

Now I use Xero software, which is automatically integrated with my customer-relationship system. When I on-board a new client, all their details get shared between the systems, and I have the ability to automatically turn a quote into an invoice between one system and the next.

My bank records are automatically pulled into Xero, reconciliation is easy, and my accountant can see the file in real time without me having to run reports. I don't need a bookkeeper anymore, and I've saved between $20,000 and $25,000 a year in costs and time saved.

Of course, both QuickBooks and MYOB now have smart, cloud-based accounting solutions, too.

Customer relationship management

Sometimes shortened to CRM, these have in the past been glorified databases, which might have looked nice but still required an enormous amount of manual work to use. Not so much now. In our business, we have a simple, cost-effective and easy-to-use CRM system, which is integrated with our marketing systems to allow us to send out emails to our client database easily and simply. All responses to emails are recorded in the clients' records in the CRM, too.

Less than twenty per cent of businesses in our ongoing survey of business owners have communicated with their existing database of customers in the last twelve months. With this technology, you'll be able to communicate and enjoy the benefits that keeping in touch with, and promoting to, existing customers will bring. Existing customers are eight to ten times cheaper to market to than prospects, so why wouldn't you?

Outsourcing/contractor technology

As little as ten years ago, we were paying up to $180 an hour for professional graphic design. Now we outsource design, and all sorts of other projects, on sites like Upwork and Elance. The jobbing, or gig, economy allows access to a wealth of talent many different tasks, globally. My most recent job was getting illustrations for this book. I used a fine-arts student in Chile, who did an awesome job for ten per cent of what the task would have cost five years ago.

Education technology

If you have staff, once thing you could find as a business owner is that you end up answering the same question dozens or hundreds of times in the course of a year. With online-course software and systems software like Enlight.io or CourseGenius, you can record and document all your key business processes, and also create short courses for your staff with videos, audio and documents.

The productivity benefit of documenting processes, and recording frequently asked questions, will blow your mind.

Cloud storage technology

When I started my first business, files were stored on disks (floppy, then hard disk), and then USB sticks. Getting artwork to the printer meant burning a copy of the disk, then booking a courier and hoping they got through peak-hour traffic to deliver it on time. Large files went sent to interstate clients via overnight courier or express postbag.

Now, with sites like WeTransfer or Dropbox, it's possible to store all files in the cloud, accessible 24/7 to all staff, customers or suppliers, to the device of your choosing. The productivity benefits for any business of document management, file transfer and the resultant drop in time and courier costs is just one aspect of the benefits of the cloud.

Chapter 9
Your Role as Business Owner

It has become common for many authors, advisers, coaches and inspirational speakers to tell business owners they have to work *on* the business as opposed to *in* the business. But it's not often that someone will actually tell you what it means.

I like to use the analogy of a toy car to explain the concept. Imagine that you're really small and driving along in a toy car. That's working *in* the business. You push the pedals, move the steering wheel, adjust buttons, and look out the window. No imagine that you are a giant pushing the toy car along. That is working *on* the business.

When you are working on the business, you are external to the business, and with a small amount of effort you can control the whole thing with just a push of your hand.

I also like to think of working on the business as setting goals, thinking about strategies, working on plans that extend beyond the horizon of an individual day-to-day task within the business.

Here are some examples of working *on* and working *in* the business:

CHAPTER 9: YOUR ROLE AS BUSINESS OWNER

- Setting an annual financial goal *versus* doing the books
- Making the decision to offer mail order as a service *versus* packaging a product for mailing
- Writing an annual business plan *versus* implementing one marketing campaign
- Considering expansion into another area *versus* interviewing staff for a new office
- Deciding on the standard of quality for products *versus* checking one product to see if it meets that standard of quality

When you start a business, naturally you are working in it. But the point of these examples is to demonstrate that your role as a business owner is to work *on* the business not *in* it. You must never lose sight of the goals, aspirations and strategies for your business.

If you ever find yourself complaining about the hectic day-to-day and not having time to plan, re-examine your role. Your first responsibility is to ensure that part of your time, intellect, activity remains outside the organisation so you can maintain perspective. Business owners who get stuck in the day-to-day are those who run their business into the ground, who miss trends in the market, and who lose out to more visionary competitors.

Working on the business is *your* job and no one else's. Sure it takes discipline to block out an hour of your time to work on the business. But a wise owl, like our friend on the front cover will never omit this no matter how tough the day to day gets. You are the engine driver, the visionary, the heart and soul, and it pays to never lose sight of this.

Speaking of being the heart and soul, let's consider your mind, body and spirit, and how you can take care of yourself as well as your business.

Chapter 10
Mind, Body and Spirit

I'm not into pop psychology. In fact, my personal opinion is that there are too many people with no training in psychology giving far too much advice to business owners. And a lot of that advice is what my grandfather used to call a 'whole lot of hooey' (dictionary definition is 'silly talk or writing, nonsense and fake assertions').

But one thing is for absolute certain. As a business owner, you need to take care of yourself. As the owner of a business, you are both the engine and the engine driver, especially early on in the life of your business. Even when you start employing people, you are the only one who will have the overall view of your goals and aspirations. You have created this entity called a 'business', and you are its mind, body and spirit.

We've talked about the difference between working in a business rather than working on a business. We've also talked a little about being a mature-age business owner. In addition, you need to take care of yourself in order to be productive in your business:

- Take time away from the day-to-day: don't get sucked into working until you burn yourself out.
- Get adequate rest; make sure you get enough sleep so you can start the day or week well rested. No doubt there will be times when you don't get enough sleep, as we all do, but try not to make this a habit.
- As we get older we can no longer eat like teenagers. Look after yourself nutritionally and take the recommendations of the experts on diet. Keep to the basics in on this. You will feel better and be more productive when you eat good-quality food. Coffee can be a good pick-me-up, but it shouldn't become a crutch that gets you started each day.
- Get some moderate exercise. I feel a million times better if I ride my bike a few times a week, and I always track more productive weeks when I have some time away from the computer. Of course, your business might already involve exercise—as opposed to my computer-based work.
- Incorporate passion and spirit into your life; do things that make you feel uplifted: gardening, watching a movie, taking your partner to dinner, or spending time with your family. I play music, bushwalk and enjoy photography. I consider these things spiritual, because I feel uplifted by them. They are guaranteed to help me get over struggles and frustrations that may drag me down. Find your passions, and your spiritual activities, and take time away from the business to invest in them.

Chapter 11
Protect Yourself and Your Business

Beyond protecting your mind, body and spirit as the business owner, there are other types of protection in business that you will want to investigate. We don't need to go into them in great detail here, but I recommend you get some expert advice on protecting yourself and your business.

I'm not a financial adviser so the following suggestions should not be taken as advice, but they are worth considering:

- Owner protection: life insurance and income protection may be important for you, depending on your financial situation. If your business is the engine room of your income, and the only avenue you have for paying off debt and funding your lifestyle, you probably should be considering this.
- Agreement protection: set up agreements with partners, suppliers or clients, and ensure that they are formally protected beyond the contents of the agreement or contract.

CHAPTER 11: PROTECT YOURSELF AND YOUR BUSINESS

- Asset protection: this covers office facilities, contents, equipment or other items important to your business operation.
- Business interruption: people often protect their business assets, but forget to protect the *operation* of the business. If the office burns down, it isn't the lack of premises that will put you out of business. It will be not being able to operate.
- Cyber risk: with technology today, and files and information on computers and apps running parts of our businesses, we need cyber protection against hackers and loss of data.

Once again, this isn't advice, but I do advise you to talk to a professional to find out what you need to protect and how.

Take-outs from Step 0

1 Are you financially ready to start a business, with reserves to keep you going for six to twelve months while you establish the business?
2 Is your business idea a winner? Have you tested it with the target audience you have in mind?
3 Are you confident that you have the structure right?

STEP 1
STRATEGY AND LEADERSHIP

Chapter 12
Your Business Model and Route to Market

Have you ever noticed how strategic an owl is? They work out exactly where the best vantage point is to see where their prey might be. Often a high tree, or the top of a building. They sit and observe for hours on end, until they spot an opportunity and swoop in on quiet wings to catch their food. In business, strategy is a very important skill to have.

It's an incredibly important part of planning your business to decide what your business model is. What does this mean? A business model is defined as the way in which a business is will generate revenue and make a profit. It can also be described as a plan for the successful operation of a business: identifying where revenue will come from, who the customers are, what products or services are for sale, and how the business will be financed.

A business model also defines the route to market, which means how the product is going to get into the hands of the customer.

You might decide to sell directly to customers online, or from your own store. Or you might decide to be a wholesaler of products to other retailers. Or you might decide to partner with other businesses. Whatever business model you choose, it has to lead to a successful operation of the business. There's no point in going to the market via intermediaries (e.g. wholesaler, agent, distributor, retailer) if the margin in the business is not great enough to support all those intermediaries.

Surprisingly, even large businesses sometimes fail to have their business model properly thought out. I've seen very large organisations that have so confused their business model that they don't even know who they are anymore. These companies tend to lose out big time because they don't have a recognisable value that they add to the market.

One particular business we worked with was trying to be the manufacturer, wholesaler and retailer at the same time. They had polluted the routes to market and were performing all of these roles: competing against their wholesalers, competing against their resellers, and eventually even competing against themselves. Separate divisions of the company were targeting the same customer and undercutting each other on quotes. Crazy.

There will be a business model that suits you, one that allows you to play to your strengths and make a profit. As we've mentioned in previous chapters, mature individuals bring with them a range of skills, experience and wisdom that can be part of the decision making process below.

Other business models may not be so successful for you, so you need to be sure to choose the one that works. Remain flexible, however, so you can adapt to competition in the market, or if your customers' needs and wants change. Here are five key factors to consider:

1   How do people buy products and services like yours now? Do they purchase locally direct from the supplier? Or is the competition from brands, which are national or local?
2   How big a scope do you have in mind? Do you want to operate in a small geographic region, such as like your suburb or city? Or

CHAPTER 12: YOUR BUSINESS MODEL AND ROUTE TO MARKET

are you thinking about operating across your state or country or even globally?

3   What resources do you have to support expansion? Many businesses run into trouble when they expand too fast and don't have enough capital or cash flow to produce higher volumes of product to satisfy market demand; or, in a service business, because there are not enough staff to deliver the services.

4   What are your strengths? If you're good at producing a high-quality, low-volume product or service, but get into trouble as soon as you have to scale up production, be careful about structuring a high-volume business model, at least until you've handled this weakness.

5   What is the current pricing/value structure of the market? Are you going to be competing head on with another business (not recommended), or creating a new niche or market position (recommended)? What margins are in the product or service for you? Can you have others resell it for you?

Chapter 13
Your Business Plan

You must have a business plan. Once you've confirmed the viability of your business idea through some initial research, you're going to need to write a business plan for it. A business plan is both a prediction of the future, and an estimate of the time, money and energy you'll need to achieve that predicted future.

Your business plan should include a summary of what you're going to do, how much you anticipate selling, and the costs associated with doing so, with a forecast profit. It will include the research you did with potential customers, plus a range of other key elements

When you write a business plan, remember that it's a document that should convince your bank manager, your investor, and of course yourself, that this crazy idea is worth pursuing and will have a positive economic benefit for you if all your plans come to fruition.

A business plan is not the place for untested dreams; it's a place for well thought out plans to bring about clear goals. Be sure to base your plan on sound ideas, judgement and data rather than on light and fluffy ideas that haven't been tested or researched.

CHAPTER 13: YOUR BUSINESS PLAN

When I write a business plan for my own business, or a client's business, I include four basic sections:

1. Executive summary: this includes the highlights of your complete plan, including your goals and aspirations with regard to financial and other measures. You should include your current situation as a way of comparing goals and aspirations with where you are now. It should also include a brief overview of the challenges and opportunities you face in executing your plan, and the actions you'll take to address these.

   Imagine you're writing the executive summary for your bank manager, or as a pitch to an investor or your board. In a few pages, give them a clear picture of your business situation and what the next twelve months look like for you.

2. Organisational plan: this is where you cover any physical or staff resources you need to execute the plan, including the existing situation, and any plans related to hiring people, capital purchases, and supply issues. Discuss things from the point of view of delivery on your promises. This is about resources, not money (covered below).

   Cover issues such as your business model; strategic relationships; legal issues like IP; any research and development you need to invest in; who does what, both in your business and externally (accounting, legal matters and insurance).

3. Sales and marketing plan: here you cover all the activities you undertake to reach out to the market and convert prospects to leads, and then to customers. Marketing activities will be about generating the leads, and sales activities will be about converting these leads.

   In this section you will also include your value proposition, strategic goals, market research, analysis. (Marketing plans are covered in more detail later in the book.)

4   Financial plan: this should include your forecasts and budget for the next twelve months, a copy of your most recent profit-and-loss statement, and your balance sheet. This section also covers cash flow and an assessment of the funding needs of the business. If you believe that your budgeted revenue and cash flow are not going to cover funding needs, or if you think you'll need additional capital for research and development, or to purchase equipment, this is where you note those plans.

This section is critical for your bank manager or finance broker. And for you also, it outlines all the plans so you can get a sense of how likely it is that you will reach your goals in the next twelve months.

I often like to include what I call 'scenario planning' in a business plan. Your budget reflects the conservative assumption of what your business will achieve, but you also need to consider any upsides and downsides to this. What if you invested more in plant and equipment? Could you sell more? What if that new competitor opened up in your suburb? Would your sales decline as a result?

No one has a crystal ball, but the more time you take to properly plan your finances for the next year, the less likely it is that you will be surprised by market changes or challenges, or any opportunities that arise.

Another thing you can include in your business plan is an appendix if you have any detailed research, information or background data that should be taken into account (make reference to it in your main business plan).

Your business plan should be succinct, concise and contain only the information that is required to plan out the year—no more and no less. If someone reading your plan wants more detailed information, they can ask for it.

TAKE-OUTS FROM STEP 1

1. Set yourself three goals for the next twelve months in your business.
2. Start writing your strategic plan or re-examine it to fill in any gaps
3. Can you think of three ways you can lead people well?

STEP 2
MANAGING MONEY

Chapter 14
Financing Your Business

We selected the owl as a mascot for this book because they are seen as wise and experienced and smart. If an owl were a business owner, they'd be a cautious yet interested one I'm sure. And when it comes to money, you certainly can do with being cautious and careful. Also, as I found in my own experience, you get better at it as you go along – once you are wise so to speak.

I mentioned previously that in large surveys, mature business owners have been proven to invest more and make more profit out of their businesses on average. This is probably in part due to their experience and cautiousness.

Before you begin to worry about how the money will flow through your business, you need to consider how you're going to finance it. As an employee, you probably never thought about the cash flow in the organisation you worked for. Each week, fortnight or month the money went into your account and your either spent or invested it from there.

In your own business, however, the timing of when money comes into and goes out of your business, and what you make on the way through is highly important. The flow of money can be unpredictable, and your job as a business owner is to put systems and processes in place to ensure it is as predictable and safe as possible.

Of course, your decisions on pricing your product, the value you offer, and the market you target all set up the initial conditions on revenue, profit and margin that will influence this over time, too. But let's look at financing the business to start with.

There are many ways to do this, and each one will either suit you or not, depending on your personal circumstances.

Bootstrapping

This is basically where you finance your business yourself from the ground up. This doesn't mean that you tip in loads of money. It's more like running a business on a shoestring, and building up your resources and the size of your business over time.

When I started my first business, I had one client, with one contract written on the back of a paper napkin. My only investments were in a desk, a computer, and a small printer. Granted, I was starting a services business so I was selling my expertise and time rather than products, but I didn't rent an office for nearly four years after starting the business, and I didn't hire my first full-time staff member for a similar time period. I was incredibly conservative with the funds I spent on the business, and this didn't happen until each client was signed up and the work had begun. In other words, I didn't spend it until I made it.

Self-funded

Although this is similar to bootstrapping, I've made them separate items. You could actually be putting in a fair chunk of your own cash, or that of close family, because you need to scale up quickly to take advantage of a market opportunity and can't wait to bootstrap it.

A little advice here: when you put on your hat as the investor rather than the business owner, make sure you are a tough investor. Do the work. Do a proper due diligence on the business idea. Don't be soft on yourself, or let yourself get away with untried and crazy ideas that are not marketable or don't meet a need. And if you borrow from family, do the same thing. Don't consider it easy money because Mum and Dad are staking you. Be as careful and cautious about their money as if it was being lent to you by the toughest of shark from the shark tank.

Cash flow

There are methods of funding your business from future cash flows. You can finance the future cash flow and give up a percentage of the 'invoice' value in what is called 'debtor' or 'invoice' financing. This can be useful if you have a fairly high-margin business but payments from clients are not coming in fast enough to fund today's operation.

But be very careful with this type of funding. Fees can be quite high—sometimes up to eight per cent for funding of a month. That's equivalent to a 96-percent interest rate on the money you've received early from 'selling' your invoices.

The company you sell the invoices to will normally take over collections from your clients, and this can result in less than perfect PR or a lack of confidence in clients who think you might be in money trouble. Personally, I don't favour this type of financing, but sometimes it can be the right solution for a particular situation.

Bank loans

Depending on the economic cycle, and how much banks want small-business business, the cost of a business loan can be relatively low, and a good way to fund a business. When borrowing from a bank, expect that they will want to see a properly presented and well thought out business plan, and maybe even some forms of guarantee from the directors of the business, such as a personal guarantee.

Once again, be very careful with what you're planning to do. Be diligent, as you'll have to pay the money back whether or not your business is successful.

Be wary of personal guarantees, and make sure you get good advice from a lawyer about them. Guarantees can often void the whole setup of a proprietary-limited company, and you could be personally liable for repayments if the structure of debt or loan, or your business, is not set up correctly.

Angels

'Angel' investors are private individuals or groups that invest in business. Generally, they do this in exchange for some equity in the business rather than as debt, which means they're risking their money for a share in your idea.

This can be a great way to get people involved in your business who have experience that complements your own. Angels will usually be quite tough on you and expect you to prepare a strong business case before they put in their money. This is good, because it will strengthen your knowledge of the business, and make the venture a lower risk for you, too.

The trick to dealing with angel investors—which can be like *Shark Tank*, only not on TV—is to make sure you have a fair and reasonable estimate of the value of your idea or business. Don't think that a brand-new idea that hasn't been tested is worth millions of dollars before you've even sold a thing. A smaller percentage of a bigger pie is better than a hundred per cent of nothing.

Don't give away the farm, either. Maybe raise the money in stages. Get enough to start, and see how the business valuation changes as you grow. You might not have to give up as much equity that way.

Venture capital

Venture capital (VC) is probably not something you'll come across. While VC shares much of the same structural idea as angel investors (VC organisations are generally bigger), they can sometimes be set up specifically to invest in opportunities that are more substantial. They generally operate at a much higher level than angel investors.

The statistics show that VC funds only one in one hundred businesses, so if VC funds your business you're in the minority. For you to receive this type of funding, the opportunity you present would have to be huge. But you should know that it is an option.

Chapter 15
Money In

There's a great saying: 'Revenue is vanity, profit is sanity, and cash flow is king.' With regard to income, it's a very accurate message. You could say, for instance, that you 'do $2 million in gross written premium (GWP)', but what counts with money coming in is how much of that is yours.

This is one of the biggest problems business owners run into. They might look at their cheque account and think, awesome, I have $20,000. And then they go out and spend that money, but the problem is that the money in the cheque account isn't all theirs.

You will probably find it difficult to look at an amount in your bank account and make an on-the-spot calculation of what is yours. You're looking at only one moment in time, and trying to make spending or investment decisions based on that snapshot. You forget that, thirty per cent of what's there is due for tax, you have to pay wages next week, you're behind on your superannuation payments, and the rent is due at the end of the month.

Then your accountant, who hasn't billed you all year, sends you a bill for several thousand dollars and suddenly you're in trouble because you just went and bought a new laptop, printer and phone system.

We could get into a whole complex discussion on how to handle this, but the simplest thing any business owner can do is set up three bank accounts for their business:

1. Trading account: this account is for anything that's needed to run the business for that week or fortnight.
2. Reserves: this set-aside account holds all your income. You might start with five precent and build it up. The idea is to, over time, have money set aside for the just-in-case moments, times when sales are slower than expected and you haven't been able to cut costs quick enough, or similar events.
3. Tax: this set-aside account is for paying tax only. Say your average quarterly tax bill from the previous year was $6,000. Each month you should put $2,000 from your income into this account as soon as it comes in from clients. If, on top of that, your end-of-year tax bill was $12,000, that's another $1,000 a month to set aside. Never touch this account for anything other than paying tax. If you don't get into the habit of putting money aside, you will run into trouble.

You could have a fourth account for super payments for staff or yourself, but the best way to handle this is to simply pay the 9.5 per cent, or whatever figure you pay additionally, on the same day that you do the pay runs. Never get behind on this or other statutory payments; they can escalate quickly and become major tax and legal issues for your business, quite apart from damaging staff motivation and morale if you don't pay on time.

If you set aside amounts dictated by a strict income policy, you'll never look at your trading account in mystery again, because you will already have set aside key expenses as soon as income comes in. By doing this, you'll also make any cash-flow holes very obvious, so you can make plans for dealing with them. Otherwise it can all be a bit of a mystery.

Chapter 16
Money Out

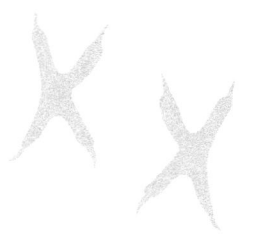

We've covered a little about money going out (also called 'outgo'). Put simply, in your business, your expenses should never be higher than your income—unless you started the business with a large investment or cash injection, and you're developing a new product or service to launch.

I always act very conservatively with expenses and only add them when I've 'sold' or closed a new deal that will lift income. Sure, on a short-term basis, market conditions may change and you may not reach budgeted monthly sales. But if you've planned badly and set up the business so that it's hampered by large expenses, and you're not doing anything about income, that's poor business management.

The second very important thing about money out is the question of *when*. You should prepare for your business a standard monthly schedule of when major expenses are due. For example, the date of your rent, the date of staff pays, the day utilities are due, the date of supplier invoice payments and so forth.

Strategically, you should try to schedule these payments for when your clients pay their invoices. In other words, don't make agreements to pay all your suppliers, rent and staff on the first of the month if you don't get paid until the end of the month.

Short-term issues might arise where cash flow is a problem, but if you've scheduled the large expenses well, a good part of your money-out situation will be under control.

Chapter 17
Recording and Reporting

Financial recording isn't difficult. It's usually just bad time management or laziness that causes businesses the most problems. I suggest you schedule in your diary time every week to wear the hat of treasurer—or chief financial officer (CFO), depending on which title you prefer.

Like it or not, you as the business owner are responsible for accurately recording the flow of money into and out of your business. To survive and prosper over time, you need the money coming in to exceed the money going out. All your income, and the value of the business, relies on this 'excess' over time.

You will want to record it accurately for yourself, but you must also report it accurately for shareholder, or the accountant, or the government, or all of these, depending on the size of your business.

Accurate recording requires the following tools and systems:

- A good accounting package: there really is no excuse these days for the 'shoebox' style of record keeping in a business. Programs like Xero and MYOB have excellent and simple-to-use programs that link automatically to your bank accounts and pull in data for you. All you,

or your bookkeeper, need to do is assign each transaction to the right 'code' or category so your accountant can prepare accurate reports and tax records. These systems have automatic reporting so they save money on things accountants used to do manually.
- Policies: write down what your policies are with regard to recording and reporting your money flow. When will you do reports? When will you (or a staff member) process invoices? When will you process payments? These policies can then be included in proposals to clients outlining your payment terms, and to suppliers with the same information. A well-written and well-communicated policy will keep everyone informed and expectations managed.
- Personal discipline: discipline is especially important in microbusiness where the owner does everything. Even if yours is a small-to-medium enterprise, where you as the owner are the CFO, you have to be disciplined and set regular times when you wear the hat of financial control, and keep recording and reporting up to date. It's easy to make excuses: you're too busy, or you have to service a client. But if you don't spend time on this, guess what? You're not actually saving time, because at some point you will have a huge backlog to get through, and every week that you miss recording, reporting and organising your money accurately, the lower your visibility and accuracy on the flow of money, and your debts and obligations, will be. And then you'll be in for a big surprise, and often a bad one.

What influences the flows?

The short answer to this question is, what doesn't? You can probably see by now that the flow of money in a business is a little like the flow of blood in a body: money sustains the business, and if the flow stops, or if you stop measuring it, you can get into a serious amount of trouble.

Your turnover is influenced by the value you offer in a market, and the quality of your marketing, product and service.

Your margin is influenced by how efficient and effective you are, and also how highly your product or service is valued, and the difference between this value and your cost of goods.

Your profit is influenced by your ability to generate income and control the costs of delivery.

Your recording and reporting, and thus visibility on the financial health of the business, are based on your systems, and your discipline in keeping everything up to date.

The overall reputation of your business is based on your ability to pay bills on time, and also on your service and product quality.

So you can see that accurate handling of the three boxes of finance—money in, money out, and recording/reporting—is a critical system in any business, small or large.

Practical exercises

1. Develop your own policies in handling money, paying attention to the following:
   - When you will invoice
   - When you will pay the bills
   - How much you will set aside for reserves and tax
   - Who you bank with, and what accounts you have to handle the above
   - Who approves expenditure in the business and to what level (sometimes called a grant of authority)

2. Develop a cash-flow schedule and a cash-flow statement for your business. The cash-flow schedule should include days of the month when invoices come in, and when supplier payments and pays are processed.

    The cash-flow statement should be for the month or quarter, and show when and how much money came in and went out, and what the net result was. Did more money come in than go out? Did more go out than come in? In the case of a new business, this will be an estimate of these things. Then you need to track what happens against your estimates.
3. Review the overall costs of your business in relation to income, and decide what you're going to do about that. Do you need to cut costs? Do you need to focus on growing income? Do you need more resources to deliver service and quality on the income coming in? Do you need to negotiate better payment terms for clients or suppliers to handle any cash-flow holes?
4. On the income side of your business, do you want to grow either revenue or profit? Write down your objectives or goals for increasing revenue, and your plans for how you might do that. For example, a marketing plan, lead generation, referrals from existing clients, selling more to existing clients, buying a book.
5. Write down some objectives or goals for growing margin, and your plans for how you might do that. For instance, price increases, value adds, selling more to existing clients, newer high-margin products, reducing production costs.
6. If you don't have the minimum three bank accounts detailed in chapter 15, I recommend that you go to your bank and set them up now. Make the two set-aside accounts interest bearing ones as, over time, you may be keeping fairly significant sums of money in them. The trading account will generally not attract interest, depending on the bank you deal with, so keep minimum funds in there to meet expense requirements as needed.

Take-outs from Step 2

1. Have you set up three bank accounts for your business?
2. Do you know your numbers?
3. Have you set a financial plan for the first twelve months?

STEP 3
MANAGING PEOPLE

Chapter 18
Business Partners and Enablers

When you run a business, you'll find over time that there's a real need for business partners and what are called 'enablers'. I'm not talking about financial partnerships, nor having a person as a director in your business. I'm talking here about people who will support you in your business. This can be a mentor, or someone you rely on to give you a hug when times are tough, or even someone who champions your cause and refers customers to you without any expectation of financial gain.

I've been fortunate to have many such people in my business-ownership life. They include my wife, who is a co-director and also someone who offers an alternative point of view. I've also had several mentors I could meet for coffee and bounce ideas off.

A good friend, who has been the chair of Blue Frog Marketing for many years, is always willing to offer a sage piece of advice, particularly by counselling me to 'cool my jets' when I get up a head of steam in a particular situation. One policy he had us institute is to give sensitive emails a 24-hour breathing space before sending. This has saved a few capital letters and exclamation marks, and probably some damaged business relationships, too.

In one episode of the TV show *West Wing*, there's a scene where the president of the United States (played by Martin Sheen) is counselling someone running for office. He asks them who will be their chief of staff, and then goes on to describe that person as a best friend, someone who has your back, who is loyal.

As a business owner, you also need someone like this. You can celebrate with them when times are great, but they'll also help pick you up when you want to throw in the towel.

Chapter 19
Suppliers

Another group of people you will have to manage and work with in your business are suppliers. If I could give you one piece of advice, beyond all the nitty-gritty of supplier agreements and so forth, it would be to choose suppliers who deliver on their promises; suppliers you can trust to deliver quality. Don't ever choose a supplier solely on the cheapest price or the fastest delivery.

Even though I make a lower margin on quality suppliers, I never sacrifice quality and trust for price. I've been bitten too many times and, conversely, my amazing suppliers have added value to my client relationships so many times.

I have used the same printer to produce large-format banners and signs for fifteen years. Over those years, the pricing for those items has changed dramatically, and it would be possible for me to have the work done much more cheaply at Officeworks or some other commercial printer. My printer has also reduced his prices over time, as technology has improved, although he is still the most expensive option. But I would never use anyone else.

Why? Because on one hundred per cent of the jobs he has done for me in the past fifteen years, I have never had cause to send back one single item for not meeting client expectations. On more than one occasion I've had to ring the printer on a Saturday or Sunday and ask for an overnight weekend print for an urgent client conference. He has never let me down.

Trust me on this. Find a group of suppliers for your business that you can work with over the long term. Build a relationship based on quality and trust, and you will never look back.

Chapter 20
Hiring, Managing and Exiting Staff

If I think of our owl once again, and imagine them as a staff member, I reckon they'd be the calm and organised type. Who went about their business quietly and got things done. They wouldn't be making a noise about it – like a cockatoo, they wouldn't be spending time chattering like lorikeets. And if there was chaos happening, they'd be the one to keep everyone and everything together.

Once you start hiring staff, you'll find it takes all sorts to build a great team, and you'll probably need to remain calm and organised like the Owl as you become familiar with getting a team to operate together successfully.

Mature people once again probably have an advantage in running businesses, because they've been through the experience of dealing with so many people in their corporate lives, they've probably developed a pretty good skill at communicating and dealing with people. They often also know the type of person they can work with effectively and easily, which gives them an advantage in hiring staff.

Of the two million or so small businesses in Australia, only 570,000 actually employ staff. Only 199,000 employ five or more staff, and only 58,000 employ more than twenty people.

In our business, we've been through pretty much every situation you can, from running the business myself to having a couple of staff, to growing to 20 staff, and then returning to a small key team with lots of tasks outsourced to external providers.

There are many reasons why businesses stay small and do not employ staff. Here's just a few:

- The business owner chooses not to
- There are not enough resources to expand
- Product or service is either very niche or not popular enough to appeal to more people
- The business owner doesn't have the skills to organise other people

We can't know for sure the specific reasons for each individual business, but what we do know from our ongoing survey of business owners is that from fifteen to thirty per cent of small-business owners rate dealing with people/staff in their business as the number-one challenge. More specifically, they have issues with finding good people, managing them, and also terminating employment. Now we're not saying you have to employ people, as you may be happy running your business on your own. But if you ever get to the point of adding to your team, we hope this chapter will come in handy.

This chapter covers some practical tips and tools you can use to improve your skills in this area. Sometimes the issue isn't about the people per se; it's simply because the business owner hasn't been trained in some of the skills, policies or procedures that will help them organise their staff.

CHAPTER 20: HIRING, MANAGING AND EXITING STAFF

Of course, the topic of people in business is broader than just staff. You'll be dealing with people as suppliers, customers, advisers, mentors and other roles in your business. It pays to have some tools to help in this area. After all, what is a business without people? Nothing.

Managing people in a business can be one of the most challenging things a business owner can do. Small businesses are often started up by one person, with that person filling the role of every job in the business for a period of time. Many business owners believe that they are the only person who can do the job properly, or do it the way they want it done. This feeling is often related specifically to the delivery division of the business. By delivery, I mean the part of the business that makes and sells the products or services of that business.

Of course, businesses have many other functions and there are many other skills required. For instance, part of the business will always be focused on planning and strategy, another part deals with the people, and yet another part handles resources like phones, buildings, and machines. A business needs to sell its products and market them, and also to make sure the quality is good. A business also needs to promote itself.

People will often start up a business because they are technical experts in delivering the product or service they started the business to focus on. They might love picture framing, or plumbing holes, or coaching staff, or saving lives. Almost as often, as good as the owner is on the technical side of things, they will be equally as bad at some of the other functions. They might get by, however, because they're amazing at their technical skill and early clients love them, willing to ignore some shortfalls like late invoicing because they love that person for their skill.

But to grow a business, a business owner will inevitably need to start handing over some of their roles to other people, either by taking on staff or outsourcing to an expert. Business owners generally start by hiring an assistant to do some office work, or another person to help go and sell product, or perhaps someone to liaise with suppliers or provide client service.

However the business grows, as soon as extra people are employed there should be a system in place for dealing with them. People management—also called human resources—can be made complicated, just like finance or marketing or quality. I recommend that you try to keep things as simple as possible. If it's simple, you as the business owner can learn it, and become competent at applying it along with all the other things you need to know as the business grows.

Business owners often want to add people to perform specific duties as a first priority. It is unlikely that a dedicated people manager will be employed until more staff have been added.

How organisations work

Here I will focus on the early days, when the business owner still has all staff reporting to them. It doesn't matter if there is one employee or ten thousand, as we discussed earlier, every business has several basic functions that need to be carried out in order to be effective, efficient, organised—and to survive.

To grow an effective organisation, the business owner is essentially handing over tasks and responsibilities that they themselves have been doing, either well or badly. As they hire more staff, they hand over more tasks and responsibilities. As the number of staff grows, each person has their own tasks and responsibilities, and these have to be coordinated. If they are not coordinated the business will not grow (this is where managing people could become complex, but I'll keep it simple).

A simple tip should serve you well in most situations. When dealing with another person, treat them fairly, respect their rights, pay them according

CHAPTER 20: HIRING, MANAGING AND EXITING STAFF

to local legislation, and respect them as a human being even when you may not agree with them, or when they haven't lived up to specific job expectations. And if you have to terminate their employment, again treat them fairly, communicate with them, and stick to local regulations.

There are only three 'boxes' in relation to managing people in any business:

- Box #1: Searching for someone new to hire and train
- Box #2: Coordinating the team that works for you
  - Box #3: Conflict resolution

Box #1: Searching for someone new to hire

Before you do any hiring of people, you must be very clear on what you are hiring them to do. This requires you to do some preparation before you have a conversation with anyone. Start by writing up a list of the tasks and responsibilities you want them to handle. Then write down how you will measure their performance of these tasks. Then write down the personal traits and skills you think they will need for that specific job.

These three items together add up to a job description and performance-management system. Once again, it doesn't need to be complicated, but it does need to be right.

If a new staff member joins your team, the basic level of respect you must have for them is to be clear on what you want them to do, and how you will be measuring their performance. If you are clear on this, it will minimise any problems down the track.

The search: In today's market there is a lot of technological support available to help you search for skilled staff. You can write and post ads on websites like Seek or Indeed. However, don't forget the old-school methods of finding good staff. Reach out to your friends, family and business network with a summary of the person you are looking for. This second method can keep the search local, and it also means that the individuals who are referred to you come with some background and recommendations from people you trust.

When posting an ad on the job network, you're basically summarising the tasks and responsibilities of the job, and how someone's performance will be measured. Of course you'll also want to tell them a little about your business, your goals, culture, and also salary ranges. But a job post needn't be any more complex than that.

You will want to make it clear whom you won't employ. Without breaching equal-opportunity laws—race, sex, religion, age (check them out for yourself)—you are quite within your rights to say, for example, that you won't employ people who are not permanent residents or who don't have a valid work visa for your location.

Reviewing resumes: Hopefully, after a couple of weeks of advising your network and posting the job on a job network, you'll have some resumes to review. Resumes can be tricky in today's market because, due to competition for jobs, some individuals may overstate their skills and competence in the hope of getting an interview. This is why I like to add a few pre-qualification questions to any job I recruit for. This is a simple two- or three-question survey that relates specifically to my business, or the role, or the individual's motivation that I can use to separate out the best candidates.

An example might be that your business deals with aged care. In that case you might ask the candidate why they want to work in aged care. In the answer you might be looking for someone who is passionate about helping older individuals, or someone who has volunteered at an aged-care home for several years.

If you work with animals, ask the candidate about their views on animals and pets. If you're in social work, ask them about any volunteering or causes they are involved with. And so on.

CHAPTER 20: HIRING, MANAGING AND EXITING STAFF

Resumes can be 'canned' information. When you challenge a candidate to think or put forward their views in a pre-qualification survey, you might find gems that match your own approach to life and work. And reduce the time you have to spend interviewing.

The interview: There is no set formula for interviewing a candidate. Really, this is just an opportunity for you to meet the person, get to know them, and ask a few questions about the role to see how they match your expectations. Remember, interviews are artificial and people can get nervous, so make the environment welcoming, be relaxed and don't interrogate them.

I usually choose between three and five people, at most, to interview. Make sure you send a quick note to anyone not selected, telling them that they have been unsuccessful. It's just common courtesy.

Alternatively, in a situation where you expect hundreds of applications, make sure you add to the advertisement the stipulation that only successful candidates will be contacted. This will serve to manage expectations.

A list of possible questions to ask in the interview you can use as a starting point:

- Ask the person about their past jobs and what they liked or disliked about them.
- Ask them to explain why they want to work for you. Look for the person who has actually researched your business or put some thought into it.
- Ask them what they do with their time outside of work. Look for people who help others, and are social. Social people generally make better employees.
- Ask a couple of questions to get the person to give you examples of when they handled a specific task or responsibility that is similar to the important ones in this job.

Always bear in mind that, depending on the role, the person may have no experience (entry level), but if the role requires specific technical skill, make sure they can actually demonstrate those skills. Depending on the role, I often set the person a practical exercise to perform that is related to the role.

Write a brief (for a marketing role), run a P&L report and comment (for a bookkeeper), review a customer complaint and comment on how you'd handle (for customer service), review a script and then do a mock call (for a telemarketer)

The selection: I usually list a few specific skill, personality and experience items I want from a successful candidate and rate each candidate out of ten in each area. I then give each candidate a total score, say, out of 70. While this isn't purely scientific, I then rank the scores and see if it matches with my gut feel on the fit of that person for the role.

I then select the top two candidates on that basis, making a phone call to the top candidate to confirm that they will accept the role. The second candidate is there in case the first has taken another job or doesn't want to proceed. I inform the other unsuccessful candidates once the top candidate has formally accepted the role and signed a letter. Not before. There are a few things that the letter of offer to the top candidate should include:

- Date of start
- Role
- Agreed salary
- Legislative benefits such as superannuation
- Breaks and leave
- Location
- Conditions

I always have a period of probation to check out new employees, and have on occasion started two people for a two-week trial and selected

CHAPTER 20: HIRING, MANAGING AND EXITING STAFF

the best based on that trial. If this is your process, be clear about it upfront so people know.

On boarding: This is an often overlooked but critical part of any hiring process. You must dedicate time to on-board the staff member. I prepare a document and file for that person prior to their start date. Included in this document:

- A copy of their contract
- A copy of their job description
- A copy of their performance-review document
- A schedule of orientation and meeting times with my staff and myself
- A guide to the local area, e.g. shops, lunch spots, public transport.

I also always make sure the desk or cubicle where that person will be working is cleaned and set up ready for them with this file, and that emails and business cards or other items are ready for them. This is basic respect stuff that will ensure the person feels welcome and knows where everything is. It also means that they will be productive much earlier than if these actions are not put into place.

Box #2: Coordinating the team that works for you

As a business grows, the owner will hand over tasks and responsibilities to individuals they previously used to do themselves. These tasks and responsibilities have to be coordinated, and nothing helps this more than the following simple set of systems:

- Weekly staff meeting: this can be a short meeting with all staff every week to coordinate what is going on. It can include a section where

each staff member shares what they are working on and what help they need from others, and for news from you as the owner/boss.
- Weekly reports: every staff member should have a template report or work in progress they prepare for you or whomever they report to. No matter how simple the job, you need to know the schedule: what has been done, and what is still to be done. In this way you can adjust for that individual by adding tasks, or helping them prioritise tasks.
- Time-management training: every staff member should be trained in simple time management, which generally involves working on the right stuff at the right time. The simplest tool for this is the urgent/important matrix. Sometimes called the 'Eisenhower matrix', the term was coined by US President Dwight Eisenhower. He famously said: 'I have two types of problems: urgent and important.' For you and your staff, this will handle a lot of upset and efficiency issues since everyone should be prioritising and working on the right stuff.
- Policies: you should have a set of general staff policies and policies for specific roles that summarise the way you do things in your business. Believe me, this will save you a heap of time having to repeat key things to people. All staff should read the general ones and also the ones specific to their job. These should be in a file on their desk, or in a public folder on your computer system and include specific items:
  - Locking up the office at the end of the day
  - When you pay suppliers
  - Who can buy stuff
  - Who you work for
  - Who can come in the office
  - When breaks are taken

CHAPTER 20: HIRING, MANAGING AND EXITING STAFF

Handling staff disputes (more on this below, in box #3). Good policies are written to help a business grow and flourish, and to stop actions and behaviours that impede and risk this growth. They are also written to free up the owner from having to repeatedly reinforce key things.

In our research, business owners constantly tell us how frustrating it is to have to repeat stuff to their staff all the time. Owners can become so frustrated with these simple processes they give up hiring people and go back to doing it themselves, which is exactly what stops them growing in the first place.

Managing a team and individuals: Somewhere in your office there should be a publicly available document that explains the overall business and individual roles in the business. It should also tell staff who to go to in specific situations. In small business especially, the business owner can end up being the place every communication or question or document ends up.

The point of creating an organisation is to hand over jobs, tasks and responsibilities so the owner is not responsible for everything. This is the purpose of communicating roles, and policies and so forth: to organise.

KPIs: While you do not share individual remuneration in a team environment, everyone should know the KPIs (key performance indicators) for each role, and the status of these KPIs for that role. Everyone should know if revenue is up or down (not necessarily profit), or if new clients have been won, or any other wins and successes.

There should be a easily seen board or poster of all your business KPIs and who is responsible for them. For example, if everyone knows Joe is the new business guy and they receive a new business enquiry, they can go straight to Joe and inform him of the details. If everyone knows Peter is the person who pays the bills, then a bill enquiry can be given to him.

Performance management: Every task, or set of tasks and responsibilities in the organisation that have been grouped together in a job must have a job description, a set of KPIs and a performance-management system. Again, keep this as simple as possible. A business owner should do the following with every team member:

- Make sure they plan their time and day based on a matrix of urgent and important to that role.
- Get weekly reports at team meeting to keep an eye on things.
- Sit down individually on a quarterly basis and go over reports and work, perhaps even giving an informal rating and suggesting actions to improve.
- A minimum of once a year, give a formal rating and tie this to incentives and or salary/income increases.

Everyone wants to know how they are doing, and how their performance relates to their growth and income improvement—or not. Never leave a staff member in the dark and then surprise them with an unexpected termination because they haven't been doing their job. That's just poor leadership and management.

Most people are social and want to do well. As the owner, it's your job to foster a good culture of growth and performance by keeping them informed and guided on their journey as a member of your team.

Box #3: Conflict resolution

Conflict is as old as life itself. No one is perfect, and from time to time people do not get along. Business owners hate conflict among staff and often feel at a loss as to how to handle it. 'I just want people to get along. After all, they are all adults,' is a common theme. It's a mystery why business owners would think this, since adults are generally more prone to fighting and holding a grudge than children. Children may fight, but they usually get over it quickly.

CHAPTER 20: HIRING, MANAGING AND EXITING STAFF

Beyond the process of conflict resolution there are some guiding rules:

- Never take up the emotion of the conflict; listen to it, but deal in facts and action. You can't handle emotion with emotion.
- Never side with the person you like the most. Remain impartial, and if you can't (if, say, a family member is involved) then get someone who can.
- Always quarantine the conversation, and make sure it's between the parties involved in the conflict (and any impartial people) only. Don't do this publicly, either in front of other staff or clients.

There are enormous amounts of resources available online, but there are five basic steps you can take:

1. Get the facts: meet the 'combatants' individually first to get their stories, but as quickly as possible bring everyone concerned together and outline the facts of the disagreement. Get understanding and agreement on the disagreement; you're not trying to resolve here, but simply to collect facts.
2. Common goals: get agreement on an outcome to the conflict the parties will work towards. It could be as simple as wanting to stop the conflict. Work with both parties to find out what they want to happen and look for commonality in those desires. Again, don't try and jump to solve unless the solution is simple; you're only trying to find common desires.
3. Reaching a goal: work with the two parties on their ideas for getting to that desired goal, and continue discussing until you've covered all the options.
4. Barriers: discuss with the parties any barriers to that goal, and also acknowledge why the conflict started in the first place. There will

be things that can be changed about the situation, and things that can't. Accept the things that can be changed and work out a plan. For the things that can't be changed, discuss ways to work around them.
5   Plan to resolve: from the first four steps, you can work out a road map to solve the conflict with both parties working on the solution. As a business owner, there may be elements where you just have to step in and resolve for them. But this is a last resort. It's your business, after all, and if after all these steps the conflict isn't resolving, or the parties are not working towards a resolution, you may have to take other actions, such as:
- Make a decision that is fair but decisive to handle or remove the conflict.
- Handle individual staff members through training, performance management or possibly termination.
- Bring in an expert to help if the above steps don't work.

Exiting staff: There are many ways in which employment in a role can end, including staff members resigning due to illness, family issues, termination due to non-performance, or changing market conditions. Small-business owners will face all of these circumstances over time when they employ staff. Some can be complicated, but try to keep things simple. For very complicated situations, I recommend that if you don't feel informed enough, or competent enough to handle the situation, bring in some short-term expertise to ensure it's dealt with correctly.

Resignation: From time to time, staff will resign. This is the natural order of things. Not being owners of the business, people will on occasion want to move to a new role, or their personal circumstances will change, or they may decide they don't like the job. It doesn't matter what the situation is, you have to handle it with respect, dignity and fairness. Most of the time it will be amicable. There are a few key things you should do:

CHAPTER 20: HIRING, MANAGING AND EXITING STAFF

- Meet the individual in a private space or location that they are comfortable with when they tell you they want to resign, and explain and the circumstances and their reasons.
- If they don't want to share their reasons, that is their right so don't push it, but if possible it's always good to do an exit interview and put it on file. This will support learning on your part, and also cover any legislative issues that could arise in the future. If you were not informed of an issue and the staff member brings it up after leaving, you can point to this interview document as evidence of good procedure (legislation is not covered in this book, so do ensure that you are informed about termination rights, and legislative rights in relation to workplace bullying and abuse).
- Quickly agree with them on timing, and announce the resignation to other staff as quickly and respectfully as possible.
- As soon as possible, give the staff member a statement of what pay is outstanding and any entitlements per their contract so they know exactly what money they will get, and when they will get it.
- Ask the individual to write up the status of all their tasks and responsibilities a day or so before they finish. And a full write up of all the tasks and jobs they do on a day to day basis – this will make it easy to get the next person grooved in. If this is overlooked, it can result in loss of information, momentum, and in some cases loss of key data like passwords to computers.
- Go over this write-up, requesting more information as needed and have the staff member then go over it with their manager, or their replacement if this person has arrived before the person leaves.
- On their final day, organise whatever social customs you need to do to give them a respectful and happy departure.

- Ensure they have handed over keys, passwords and other work-related items like computers and phones before they leave the premises for the last time.
- Don't leave things undone on the last day. Ensure that the change is ordered and clear-cut for all concerned.

Change of conditions termination: As a business owner, especially in a small business, you could be forced to terminate a staff member due to changing market conditions. Sales may have collapsed and you can't afford to keep someone on. In this situation, you need to cover all the items related to a resignation as well as one other very important thing: you must clearly inform the staff member of the reason for the termination, and ensure they know it is not personal or performance related. Never use changing conditions as a reason to hide performance-related termination.

Performance-related termination: Sometimes a staff member simply can't do their job, or they don't fit in, or they cause trouble. All these circumstances are performance related. Legislation exists to protect individual staff members from unfair dismissal, but the business owner also has rights in relation to performance. I'm not covering legislation here, but I do offer some simple advice in these situations:

- Handle the situation early: don't let difficult or underperforming staff wreck your business by letting it go on too long.
- Check your own backyard: have you given the person the right training? Is there a personal issue that is causing them distress and impacting performance? Is another staff member the source of the problem?
- Keep records of everything: if the issue is specifically performance related, then you need to know the regulations and follow them,

CHAPTER 20: HIRING, MANAGING AND EXITING STAFF

and you need to keep notes on every conversation you have with that individual. Other than these notes, follow all the other steps that make sense from the resignation or changing circumstances section above.

- Security: secure keys, passwords, computers, and phone.
- Basic respect: treat the individual with respect even if they are causing trouble. You need to have private conversations with them. Be clear that they are being terminated for performance-related issues and explain exactly what those issues are. And give them a copy of any documentation you're keeping on that issue. Again, check legislation for specifics.
- Discretion: unless specifically required because of the person's role, you don't need to inform other staff of the specific circumstances or reasons for that person's leaving. In fact, it's best not to. This shows respect to the individual, and also protects you in any legal situation.

Take-outs from Step 3

1 Who are the people you need to manage in your business: suppliers, partners or staff?
2 What are three things each staff member must be given?
3 Check your local employment and OH&S (occupational health and safety) legislation and any other legislation specific to your industry.

STEP 4
MARKETING AND PUBLIC RELATIONS

Chapter 21
The Importance of Value

Value is probably the most important concept to get to grips with when running a business. If you don't have something of value to offer a potential customer, you probably won't be able to make a profit on your product or service. The higher your service, the higher your profit. And in the absence of value, business owners often find they can complete in only one area: price.

Understanding value

The first step in the journey of value is to understand exactly what value means. In this part of the marketing process you're exploring what customers value in relation to a specific product or service. And in relation to this, how well your business is placed to deliver a product or service that matches or exceeds the value they are looking for.

In the same context, since there is competition in pretty much any market, you need to know how well your competitors are delivering on this value as well. The way you find out about what people value is, not surprisingly, by asking them.

You can search for information that already exists, and no doubt people will have done research on the same market or product in the past. This is often called 'available' or 'secondary' research and can often be available from industry groups and associations and from the Bureau of Statistics in your country. Or you can conduct your own surveys with people in your target audience. This is often called 'primary research'.

To be a successful business owner, you need to understand the value that is required by the customer, the value you can deliver, and how your value compares to others who are also targeting that same customer.

A wise owl, like our friend on the cover of this book has very very good hearing, and he listens carefully, and I'd recommend you take a leaf out of his book when it comes to understanding value in your customers – listen to lots of them, and you'll learn what counts.

Creating value

Once you've done some research in your business and you have a handle on your own business, your ideal customer, your competition and the market itself, you can begin the process of creating value.

Value is simple in concept, but the devil is in the details. It doesn't matter if your business is product or service based, you will be aiming to embed in that product and service the things the market and your potential customers tell you are needed and wanted. And it isn't just the product or service itself that contributes to this value; it's also business systems like the following:

- How easy it is to order from you

- How well your marketing messages communicate the value you offer
- Whether or not your staff are easy to deal with when they answer the phone
- Your returns policy

As a starting point, you almost want to have a checklist of all the things you know are valued by your potential customer. Then you can check these off one by one as you develop your product or service. Some things may be more or less expensive for you to embed into your product or service, and you may have to make trade-offs in regard to what you eventually deliver.

Remember, when creating your value proposition the success of your business will rely on how well you've matched the needs and wants of your customer in the process. Nothing more, nothing less. Don't get caught up in making assumptions about what they will value, nor in over engineering your product or service so it isn't profitable for you to deliver.

Here's an example of a value proposition to assist you:

John's butcher shop offers its customers – who are health conscious families with a high disposable income, high quality organic meat. Our promise to our customers is our meat is certified and fresh, and we add value by giving every customer an extra piece of meat in every order.

Delivering value

Delivering value isn't just about the physical delivery of a product or service. Of course, it is important, and many companies get this wrong by making a promise and failing to deliver on it. How many complaints have you heard recently about a telecommunications company, airline or bank? Every complaint means there was a failure to deliver on an expectation or promise.

In this value step, there are two key elements: physically delivering the product or service; and checking that the delivered product or service is as expected and valued as it should be.

Chapter 22
The Seven Principles of Successful Marketing Organisations

Something that is very common about businesses that are stuck in a rut, or don't know what to do with their marketing to obtain growth, is that they're not organised around the customer. In this chapter, we review the seven principles that will help fuel your success in marketing your business.

Principle #1: Organise around the customer

Have you ever walked into a business in a retail environment and stood around waiting for ages to be served, even though employees were sitting at their desks within view of you without looking up or acknowledging you? Not their job. Sometimes it can feel like they're actively avoiding you while they do something that's obviously highly important on their computer or desk. You know the feeling.

Look at the organisation chart of most businesses and most job functions or responsibilities are organised around the leader of a business, or a particular department. The very look and feel of an organisation chart is one of fixed structure—stuck boxes. There is no flow, other than up and down among the staff. Consider a more circular model, where the customer is at the centre of the circle, or the focal point of an eye. Here, all the activities of the business are visually, physically, philosophically and actionably organised around the customer.

I've found that walking into Officeworks in the last few months has been a completely different experience than in the past. There is someone at the entry to greet customers, and almost every staff member looks the customers in the eye and says hello. These people are obviously there to serve you. They are not pushy, but they're definitely aware of you and respectful of your presence.

The same goes for the VicRoads office. My past experience was of a very bureaucratic organisation, and I actually felt like I was in a government department. But recently, when I walked in to register my new car, there was a bright, bubbly, smiling concierge to greet me, ask me what I needed, and direct me to a very specific location in the office where I got rapid and friendly service. Yes, I still got a number from a machine and there was still a short wait, but the greeting and the directing was a perfect way to acknowledge that I was here, and I was going to be served professionally.

Key attributes of businesses that are organised around the customer:

- They survey regularly.
- They're super quick to answer phones, emails, complaints, enquiries.
- They're friendly and professional.

- They quickly acknowledge when they've made a mistake and fix it for you, sometimes even going beyond just the fix to add value.
- They add value in transactions.
- They know their product and can help you.
- They are observant, acknowledge your presence, and ensure there are other friendly human interactions.
- Their process, from your first enquiry to doing business to deliveries, is clear, friendly and professional.
- Their products and services are exactly as promised.
- They are human and make mistakes, but they fix them.
- They don't put bureaucracy or barriers in the way of helping you.
- Their offices and premises are clean, inviting and easy to navigate.
- They are easy to do business with.
- They know your needs and wants implicitly.
- They know you.

Principle #2: Search for understanding

In today's world, it seems many businesses are getting further and further away from their customers, and more and more insulated inside themselves. In both of our businesses, we have surveyed more than twelve hundred business owners, and found that less than twenty per cent seem to be interested in what's going on with their customers in terms of needs and wants, or trends in their marketplace, or how competitors are changing their strategies or campaigns.

Running a business is tough, and there is a lot of pressure on business owners and staff to get the day-to-day tasks done in their job. They often feel like they don't have time to work on the business, and while this may be a fact, it can also be used as an excuse.

A business that is disconnected from its market, customers and competitors, or even its own position in the market, is far less likely to survive than a business with a thirst for understanding. To do otherwise is leaving future prosperity, success or even survival to chance. It's blaming conditions or 'the way it is' for not being in touch with the surroundings, which, in a business sense, equate to market, customers and competitors.

Imagine trying to get up from your desk at the office and making it all the way home with a blindfold and a set of noise-cancelling headphones on. You might find it pretty hard, and in fact it might be incredibly dangerous. Consider the equally dangerous situation of running a business with no awareness of what is going on.

Having a thirst for knowledge and understanding is a mission-critical skill for any business owner. It keeps them on top of the trends, aware of customer needs, and conscious of what the competition is doing. It isn't hard, and there are many simple tools for researching a market, surveying customers, and observing competitors. But it isn't an option. And there are no excuses. It must be done for a business to survive and prosper.

Principle #3: Be selective

In today's economy, business owners can sometimes feel a sense of information overload. Content marketing is all the rage, and along with customer communications, financial communications, staff communications, at times it can all seem too much and cause a business owner to reject all the information, or feel tired and irritable at having to handle another piece of data.

Successful business owners are selective. They have in place policies and procedures to separate the important from the unimportant in their business. This isn't necessarily a skill that is native to a human being. We have five senses and they are turned on all the time. Sure, we could shut our eyes, or we could put on headphones, or we could just zone it out. And sure, some people are good at concentrating in noisy situations. And some people do in fact wear headphones on their way to work or school to cut off some of these information flows.

However, the downside to this is an absence of important information. I'm sure you've seen someone with headphones on walk out in front of traffic, or walk into another person on the street because they weren't fully aware of their surroundings.

In business, you must have full awareness of what is going on, but you also need the ability to separate out the important stuff. You want the best of both worlds.

Putting aside your innate ability to do this, there are many strategic business tools that can help you select the important from the unimportant and make decisions based on that information. Tools designed for that purpose include SWOT analysis (which stands for strengths, weaknesses, opportunities and threats) and PESTLE analysis (also spelled PESTEL), which stands for political, economic, social, technology, legal and environmental trends. Segmenting a market and selecting a target customer group is a strategy that is also designed to help a business focus.

Using tools like this will give a business owner what seems like the superhuman ability to run a focused and profitable business—superhuman to those business owners who aren't aware these tools exist and live their lives running from one urgent task to another, never finding a priority focus to help them prosper in their business.

The successful business owner is able to be selective, and as a result enjoys an environment that is far more under their control than others who can't focus, or don't have the tools to focus their energy.

Principle #4: Seek truth

Many business owners are operating off assumptions about their customers, business and market that are out of date, incomplete or just plain wrong. They can hide behind assumptions all they like, and they can hope for the best in a business, but unless they know the true value of what they do within the context of customer needs and wants, and in comparison to what else is available in a market, they will not survive for long.

History is littered with examples of both market segments and individual businesses that held onto out-dated assumptions, product offerings or solutions, and were passed by due to changes in needs, behaviours, government or other factors.

We no longer use the horse and buggy because cars came along, but I'll guarantee you that somewhere on the planet at that time was a business that stubbornly clung to the hope that those damned infernal smoky automobiles would never last.

More recently, witness the desperate moves by taxis to block Uber drivers via legal action. Prior planning, preparation and understanding of customers may have reduced the impact of Uber. Taxis could have 'Ubered' themselves before Uber even arrived.

If a business owner operates a business centred on the customer, has a thirst for knowledge, and is able to select the important facts and information from the data available to them in a market, they will be able to identify a truly valued position for themselves in any marketplace.

What is truth in terms of value? Simply put, it's a market position that can be secured and defended. It's the ability of a company to deliver a profitable, valuable solution to a specific type of customer and have them want to buy it at volumes that will enable the business to make money and grow. It's also having the resources available to meet the goals and objectives of the business in relation to delivering that product or service to that target audience.

Business owners who utilise this truth in their business will survive more effectively and controllably than those who don't. Those without their own business truth are relying on luck and happenstance for their survival and are not in control of their destiny.

Principle #5: Be open

A business owner who knows their own truth is one thing, but many businesses don't do anywhere near enough to let their customers, prospects and market know what they have to offer.

In our business-owner survey, less than twenty per cent of companies have a written marketing plan. Less than fifteen per cent have communicated to existing customers. Less than five per cent measure which type of marketing works.

In short, companies underestimate and underdo what is required to grow their businesses profitably. Sure, many are reasonably successful and get referrals, but many are doing less than they could with a strong program of communication to the market, prospects and customers.

Many companies also lose a fair percentage of their customers each year, a phenomenon called 'churn rate'. This means they have to find quite a few new clients just to retain their sales or profit from the year before.

A habit of openness, or, if you like, willingness to communicate about the company to the market, customers and prospects is a prerequisite to continued growth, profitability and survival.

These six elements are common to businesses that practise openness:

- They have a marketing plan and communicate to customers regularly – even chatting to customers as you serve them you can learn a lot. They also promote to new prospects and the wider market through social media and other activities like letterbox drops
- Someone is responsible for the marketing activity – if you're running the business yourself, just schedule a little time each week to focus on this and keep it simple
- The business has a clear idea of their value and how to communicate it to customers.
- These businesses deliver on their promises to customers in relation to this value. In other words, received value (after purchase) is at least as good as perceived value (prior to purchase).
- These businesses grow in relation to their market. Markets grow fast or slow, but an openly communicating business will usually grow faster than the average in their particular market.
- There are tools, procedures and systems that support open communication: visible signage, working phone systems, emails that get answered, an interest in customer feedback, and a willingness to solve any issues that arise

Principle #6: Measure

In the old Western movies, you sometimes saw a person put their ear to the train tracks or ground to listen for an approaching train or riders on horseback, the theory being that they could hear the sound in the metal or ground before they could actually see the train or horses.

The saying 'keeping your ear to the ground' comes from this, and the habit is incredibly important in business. No, I don't mean putting your ear to the floor in your office. I mean using some sort of method to listen to the market or your customers, or some kind of measurement to find out what approach to marketing is working.

A business that has its ear to the ground will be more successful than one that doesn't because it will be more aware of the environment, and also knowledgeable about successful and unsuccessful actions in their business.

There are many, many ways you can measure your marketing strategy. Here are five habits for successfully measuring the performance of your marketing:

1   *If you can't measure it, don't do it:* John Wanamaker supposedly said, 'I know fifty per cent of my advertising is working, I just don't know which fifty per cent.' I personally reject this situation, as I can't afford to waste half my investments in my business, and I'm sure you're the same. This is why I advise clients to work out how to measure a marketing program before they commit to it. And if they can't work out a simple measure, I would advise them not to do it.
2   *The golden question,* which is one of the simplest and most important marketing measures: 'Where did you hear about us?' In an instant, this gives you a guide as to what marketing has delivered that customer to you. And if asked over time to many customers, the answers will give you a trend for the best channel to be promoting yourself.

    Some so-called experts claim that the customer won't remember. Maybe they saw a few different ads in different places before coming to you. Frankly, I don't care. Whatever ad or promotion they remember is the one I will increase my investment in, and if that's the one that brought them in, I'm happy to use that as a measure. This question should be a critical step in any first contact discussion with a new customer.

3   *Measurement by observation:* you don't have to survey customers or prospects to get information about what people like and don't like. You can simply observe them in a shopping centre. We've conducted many surveys for clients in food courts and shops, simply observing how people move through a store or location, what they interact with, and how they choose a store.

   If you have a retail store, stand in the store and simply observe people. You may find out some interesting information about where to place advertising, point of sale, and which products to keep or discard. There are many ways to build knowledge, information and measure your marketing.

4   Return on investment (ROI): this simple calculation adds up sales from a marketing program and divides this figure by costs to get a ratio. For example, if you make a twenty-per cent margin on revenue, you need a ratio of $5 for every $1 invested to break even. For example, let's say it costs you $8.00 to make a picture frame and you sell it for $10.00, you're only actually making $2 in margin. If you spent $20 on marketing, you'd have to sell $100 of frames before you even started making any money. In our marketing business, we have in the past changed marketing programs and compared alternative campaigns, and found differences of up to twenty times on ROI for the same investment. Using this comparison means you can prioritise where to spend your marketing dollar.

5   *What measures success:* a good habit is working out what success looks like for a campaign before you start it. For example, a customer is worth $500 to you on average. Let's say you were looking at running a Google campaign for $5,000. You can say that you would need at least ten customers for that campaign to break even. If you look at that campaign and think it unlikely you will get ten customers, then you can decide whether to do the campaign in the first place.

Principle #7: Adapt

Charles Darwin said, 'It is not the strongest of the species that survives, nor the most intelligent that survives. It is the one that is most adaptable to change.' Personally, I like this saying a lot. Strength and intelligence are fine attributes to have in a business or marketing sense. However, as many business owners know from experience, the only constant in business is change.

Unfortunately for many businesses and categories in markets, it seems like the game is to find a way to do something and then keep doing it as long as possible, resisting change until there's no other solution but to go out of business or jump on the new way to do it.

Businesses can't be blamed for this. Often a lot of investment goes into infrastructure to manufacture products in a certain way, or a lot of investment goes into training staff to deliver services in a particular way. They just get comfortable and then some damn fool comes along and changes the playing field.

That is just the way of life in business. And the pace of change due to technology and the interconnectedness of the world through the internet are only going to get faster. Years ago, people may have done something in a certain way, oblivious to the fact that another culture had a much easier way to do the same task on the other side of the world. Today, literally minutes after someone finds a new solution, with one post on social media the whole world can know about it.

So there is a lot of truth in the fact that a successful marketing business will need to be adaptable to survive in the future. This doesn't mean that people will buy insurance in a different way every single day, but the pace of change will speed up, and this has to be taken into account when working out investments in machines, people, premises or other resources. It will impact how long to sign supply agreements for, and it will influence the type of people employed. It will influence a lot of things.

So here's the practical consideration in relation to this principle for survival: make sure you keep connected to customers so you know what they need and want, and how this changes over time. Make sure you don't get stuck in your ways in relation to these changing needs, or the changing strategies of your competition or the market. Make sure you're not tied to fixed-condition suppliers of products or services for your business. Also, choose adaptable partners.

Make sure you hire staff that can handle change as it occurs without freezing like a deer in the headlights if they're asked to learn a new app or piece of software. Make sure you have business plans, policies; structures in place that support being adaptable as opposed to being fixed to one approach in your market.

Chapter 23
Being a Good Corporate Citizen

At some stage in the launch and running of your business, you'll want to let the world know about the good things you're doing. In this chapter I cover public relations (PR) and how to get other people to talk about you. PR is one way of doing this. In simple terms, PR means getting someone else to talk about you in unpaid media as opposed to you paying for advertising and other promotions, where you're generally talking about yourself.

In research, mature people are often more engaged with the concept of their impact on the world and the community in which they live. Whether it is age or experience or because they have elderly parents or teenage kids, but they are often quoted as feeling a sense of duty, or have started thinking about what legacy they want to leave. This is a great viewpoint to have when thinking about how your business can both make money, and do well.

There are many angles to PR. What isn't generally well known is that both referrals and word of mouth are actually PR, not marketing. So getting testimonials or having someone else tell another person about you is a public relations activity.

You may have heard the term 'good corporate citizen'. This is related to work done by a business beyond its products and services in a community to help out. Often companies will publicise their good-corporate-citizen activities to enhance the perception of their brand in the marketplace. Sometimes this is seen as self-serving, but I find that attitude quite cynical—although it is sometimes true in rare circumstances. The reality is there actually are a lot of good-hearted business owners out there who just want to make a difference and give something back.

Over many years, my businesses have undertaken various unpaid activities in the local community, and also donated to social-betterment programs. You may feel inclined to do the same way, too.

Some of the things we've done in our public-relations program:

- Sat on boards
- Given pro-bono advice to community groups
- Welcomed marketing interns into our business for work experience
- Given away copies of our books to charities for them to sell
- Donated to charities and social-betterment programs
- Made free subscriptions to our marketing resources available to charitable groups

Even if your motives are not self-serving, it would benefit you to make people aware of what you do. At Silver & Wise, we publicise some things, and keep other things private. The balance between what you talk about and what you keep private is up to you.

If you decide to do something in the community, make it something you love doing. But there can be a commercial element to community partnerships, and I encourage you to consider this option if these partnerships operate at a local level. It can be an incredibly valuable marketing tool to set up community partnerships, much like Ritchie's IGA does with their community benefits cards. I even wrote a book on the subject, advising community groups on how to set up partnerships with business owners. The book is called *Raising Dough*, and one hundred per cent of the profits go to community groups.

We've run successful community partnerships in real estate, banking, insurance and retail restaurants, so we know it works. If you focus on groups where members are in your target audience, this can be even more powerful, and can result in a local community that adds strong support to your business in a competitive environment—you are giving back something from patronage they bring to you.

Always do this as a donation for business, not as sponsorship. If you want to donate to a charity, or do sponsorship because you like a group, go right ahead, but if you want a commercially measurable partnership, donate *after* you have been given the business. Consider this distinctly separate from charity, something you do because you want to and don't expect a return.

Word of mouth is the most powerful form of promotion in a business. It's others talking about you, and not you talking about yourself. But it takes organisation and willingness to deliver on your promises to make it work for you. Many, if not all the parts of the business can contribute to word of mouth – from effective sales people, to good customer service, to delivering on your promises. From providing good quality, to only promising what you can deliver in your marketing.

Chapter 24
Getting Customers to Talk About You

Most businesses end up with a small percentage of customers they class as priority A, or top customers because they buy a lot, or buy regularly. Another element that can define the importance of a customer is whether they refer others to the business or advocate that business to others. This customer takes on additional value because they influence the purchase decisions of others. This can be the mum who brings friends to a particular cafe every week, or the accountant who refers people to an insurance brokerage.

These advocates are special people. But how do you get them, and how do you get them to talk about you? The first thing is to deliver on your promises, as discussed previously. You have to deliver well on what you said you'd do, and perhaps even do a little more than expected for that person.

You can certainly ask good customers if they would refer you, and their willingness to do so will be dependent on the previous point. But

CHAPTER 24: GETTING CUSTOMERS TO TALK ABOUT YOU

sometimes people won't think about doing this unless you ask. We call these 'activated' referrals (as opposed to 'passive' referrals). Many people will refer you if you remind them that you need new business—without sounding desperate, of course.

Some business owners think this referral has to be incentivized. For example, tell a friend and we'll give you both a $20 shopping voucher. This isn't the case at all, but a thank-you is even better than a please. This means that if you do get a referral, I recommend that you send a thank-you note, or maybe a bottle of wine, or even some of your product to that person as a simple thank-you for referring someone. You could also consider the option of giving a donation to their favourite charity or community group they belong to. In any event, letting them know how much you value their custom and their advocacy is a nice way to approach this.

Chapter 25
Getting the Media to Talk About You

Media doesn't just mean national TV, radio, TV or printed publications, or even international media. While that might be good for the ego, there may not be a lot of point to being in a national TV show if you only operate in one suburb in Sydney.

Before we get into more detail, I want to encourage you to seek out media with your new business. There is a real and escalating interest in mature entrepreneurs and business owners in the current market. I'm not certain why, but maybe it is a relatively new phenomena and journalists want some balance to talking about the latest tech wunderkind. Anyway, there is an opportunity for you to take advantage of in the market.

I'll quickly introduce the concept of targeting here. The reason you might want a profile in the media is that it will help people get to know about you, and also provide very valuable exposure that you might not be able to otherwise pay for. But if you operate an aged-care business in the local area, it can be just as valuable and sometimes a whole lot easier to get PR exposure in the local newspaper, or even on local community radio.

There are many methods of running a successful PR campaign. I interviewed Jules Brooke, the founder of Handle Your Own PR (handleyourownpr.com.au) for some tips. Here is what she recommends:

- Look in local papers to find out which journalists are writing stories in your market segment or to your target audience demographic. They may be interested in crime stories and you have a security business. They might write about aged care and you have a local in-home help service. They might write about kids' parties and you have a party shop. You get the idea.
- Build a list of these reporters/journalists or online bloggers. Contact them and ask what interests them about your type of business or activity. You might also ask if there's a topic they're interested in writing to guide you.
- Write a short publicity release that is appealing to a specific journalist covering information about you that is relevant for their readership. Keep them up to date with more interesting information, such as activities your business has completed, new technology, successes and wins, work in the community you've done etc.

Many small-business owners think that a special promotion, or the opening of a new store, or other 'sales' messages are interesting PR, but they are not. The average journalist or editor probably receives dozens if not hundreds of releases a day and the ones that stand out will have something interesting to them beyond the sales message. Keep your sales messages for your paid advertising.

And please also try not to be a bore. PR is not about you being famous or preening your feathers. Owls don't make showy presentations.

But they do present well. Getting good PR doesn't require you to carry on like a 'two-bob' watch.

The world has changed, and journalists are no longer the only influencers in markets. There will be many target-specific bloggers online who have built a strong following in your market. Your approach to these people should be the same: find a relevant blogger, contact them and follow the process outlined above.

Don't expect them to just jump at writing about your brand new pink sneakers or the introduction of a "camel hair latte". Build a relationship and see how you can work together on ideas of mutual interest.

Take-outs from Step 4

1. Do you understand your value proposition?
2. Do you have a marketing plan?
3. How are you going to get the word out?
4. What could you do in your business to be a good corporate citizen?
5. Is there anything specific that you can do to ensure that customers will rave about your business?
6. Do you have an idea for a special story about you or your business that is newsworthy, even at the local-newspaper level?

STEP 5
SALES AND BUSINESS DEVELOPMENT

Chapter 26
Your Target Audience

Salespeople in a business are often known by their activities, but not how important they are in the flow of income into a business. The fact is, no income flows into a business to pay for stuff, or keep people in jobs, unless someone with a sales role identifies, meets and convinces a prospect to do business with the organisation.

When you start out in your business, the salesperson is you. In larger businesses, the general manager or sales representative may do it. In some industries, it's a very technical role with high levels of product knowledge required. In others it's a fast-paced, high-pressure, gift-of-the-gab type of role.

No matter who does it, or the intricate style of the role in for a particular industry, the purpose of sales and business development is very clear and very simple. It is to convert someone who doesn't do business with an organisation into someone who does. And then over time to increase the amount of business that person does with the organisation through repeat purchase, or cross-selling additional products and services.

A sales person deals in one-on-one situations, whereas marketing departments tend to deal in groups: a target audience or market segment. It's the salesperson that meets with an individual, and through a series of conversations brings them to the point where they decide to buy. It's the salesperson that does the deal. It is the salesperson that has to use communication skills on a one-to-one basis to convert the prospect into the customer.

Most importantly, it's the role of the salesperson to start the financial relationship with a customer. Marketing might start the awareness, or the reach, or the education, but marketing doesn't actually make the sale.

The information in this section will help you build an understanding of all the steps of the sales process. It will help you organise your sales activity so it's working well and is supported with resources. It will cover the key skills you need as a salesperson.

Once again, if I may comment on the mature individual. It is my belief that by the time you get to your 40's and beyond, you've probably worked out that you can often find out more and learn more by listening that you can if you are talking. You've probably made mistakes in talking too much at times, or been counselled by a manager in a job that you hadn't listened. You've developed over time strategies for understanding people and their needs, so these skills will stand you in good stead as a salesperson.

If you are the business owner as well as the salesperson, this information will inform you and give you a framework to operate from. If not, it will make you aware of the skills your salesperson will need, and help you hire and train that individual.

What this information won't do, however, is make a sale. For that to occur, you have to take the information and either practise it or ensure that your salesperson is competent in it and/or practising it.

Sales only come from knowledge that is practised, thereby enabling the knowledge to be applied to a successful conclusion—the sale. So don't expect to read this chapter and become the perfect salesperson, because it won't do that. The contents of this chapter will provide you with the knowledge to practise and become effective in the function.

With finance, you can learn the skill and then independently complete a profit and loss, or process an invoice, or work out your cash flow. For sales and business development to work, you have to apply it to another human through conversation (specifically, listening) and objection handling. The information can provide you with the tools, but if you don't use the hammer it will never work for you.

Sales focus

It's quite amazing to consider how much time salespeople can waste by conducting the sales process with 'prospects' that are not the target market of the organisation. If a business has a very specific target audience, it's important that the salesperson or sales team knows what it is, and focuses their energies on converting from within that target audience.

The same principle applies to marketing budgets; they also need to be focused and targeted. If salespeople are all over the place, talking to anyone who will listen, their efforts will result in lower rewards.

There's nothing wrong with identifying a new niche, but before a whole sales effort is put into that niche, sales need to hand the idea back to the business to test against strategic goals and objectives. A salesperson should be calling on the agreed target audience and *only* the agreed target audience.

Chapter 27
Steps in the Sales Process

Every business owner needs to be a great salesperson or employ someone else who is a great salesperson to sell, confidently and effectively, all products and services relating to the business. There are many steps in the sales or business-development process, the most important of which I cover in this chapter. Without the ability to sell your product or service, you will find it difficult to start and run a successful business.

When I use the word 'identity', I'm referring to the individual person, prospect or customer you deal with in your business. I use this word specifically because it has the extra meaning of not treating someone as a number. Each potential customer should be treated as a real person, i.e. an identity.

The individual identity within your ideal target audience

If a business is well organised and focused, it will have a target audience. Your marketing will be well targeted, and *leads* will be coming into your business from that target audience. For each individual lead, the salesperson should have a process in place regarding the information that must be handed over from marketing, including:

- Name
- Phone
- Email
- Address
- Enquiry/need

For instance, in the insurance industry a lead usually includes the above information, plus an agreement from that customer confirming that they want a quote on their insurance. It should also include an expiry date for their current insurance. If all this information is not present, it's not a lead but simply an enquiry.

Some sort of system is necessary for capturing and entering this data as a lead/prospect; for example, a spread sheet, database or customer-relationship management (CRM) system for capturing and entering each identity as a lead or prospect. Possibilities include Salesforce or Zoho, but there are many others.

Setting up an appointment

After the information on a lead is captured and recorded, and the lead is accepted as genuine, the next step in the sales process is setting up an appointment. Naturally, this means calling or emailing and agreeing on a mutually suitable time to call or meet. And also naturally, this requires a system of appointment scheduling, or a calendar of all appointments.

Time and resources are often limited. In smaller businesses or when you are first starting your business it might be you making this call or meeting, so it's important at this stage to check the qualification/enquiry. This is sometimes referred to as 'pre-qualification' and may involve a further step of checking the 'quality' of the lead.

In the property-investment market, some businesses ask the prospect or lead to fill in a questionnaire detailing their income, financial position, purchase timing and other information. This allows the business to gauge whether it's worth spending time on a call or meeting, or if the person should be handled through means other than a one-on-one call. Depending on the business, it might be that they need more information, or they don't qualify to buy a property, or they simply want to buy insurance that the company doesn't have, or a product it doesn't stock.

In any event, pre-qualification is an important consideration for businesses with limited resources to avoiding wasting time and resources on someone who doesn't qualify.

Pre-work

Assuming a prospect gets through the qualification process and an appointment is set up, the salesperson should have a process of pre-work:

- Find out about the company.
- Find out about the prospect.
- Find out about the location.

Anything that will help improve the chance of converting the prospect into a customer should be done prior to the call. This information should all be added into the notes on the customer and used by the salesperson to prepare for the first meeting, as a professional would naturally do.

Going into a call not knowing about the person, business or location could waste resources and, in a business-to-business situation, make the salesperson seem unprofessional or uncaring.

Pre-call

Separate to pre-work, there is also a very specific pre-call routine a salesperson should go through before going on a call. At a minimum, the salesperson should ask themselves these important questions:

- Do I have all the brochures, presentations, tools I need including pen and notepaper?
- Do I know where I'm going?
- Have I got enough time to get there early?
- Do I have my business cards?
- Are my shoes and teeth clean?
- Is my uniform/suit tidy?
- Do I know the information I researched?
- Do I know the name of the person I'm meeting?
- Have I confirmed that the time is still okay with them?

All this pre-work can add to professionalism, timeliness, and good first impressions.

Exercise: Write up a checklist for your own business. Use the above as a guide, but make it relevant to your specific business.

The appointment/sales call

Once all the above has been taken care of, the next step is the actual appointment/sales call. As previously mentioned, a book can't make a good salesperson. It can supply the tools, make suggestions, and encourage certain systems and behaviours, but becoming a good salesperson takes practice and, frankly, lots of sales calls. Some will make you want to vomit afterwards, some will be bad, some will be okay, and some will be *awesome*. Over time, the percentage of *awesome* calls will start to grow.

However, putting your skill aside, there are systems and procedures you should have in place to help the actual sales call go well.

Introduction

You should have a well-rehearsed and smooth introduction, and your business card ready to hand over. Do the usual human things: be respectful and polite, acknowledge the person, look them in the eye, be friendly. You know the drill.

Have your questions prepared. Have an opening that gets them talking as soon as possible. You could start by thanking them for the opportunity to talk, and then summarising what you believe they asked about to confirm the details/scope of the meeting.

Take a moment to orient yourself to the room or office you are in. Find out about the person and, importantly, identify things you like about their office, location and room. This will help you be more authentic and build rapport with them.

It's always useful if you share an interest in common, whether it's volunteering, golf, or kids. It's said that people do business with those they like, so if you share a genuine interest in something it will contribute to that affinity or rapport. Don't ever force this. Don't say you like golf if you don't. People hate fakers, so be genuine.

Encourage the person to agree/adapt/add to what you've said.

Structure the meeting around listening, particularly the first meeting. Ask the questions you need to clarify their needs. Listen carefully and take notes as necessary.

Answer their questions honestly, openly and briefly. Don't waffle on unless the customer wants more details. Make sure you summarise the conversation, and be clear on what you're going to do for them at the end.

Pitching

The end of the sales call may be a sale, it may be an agreement to submit a proposal, or it may be scheduling a next meeting. Whatever the next step, don't force things too fast, but at the same time don't miss the opportunity to close if that seems like the thing to do.

The point about sales is that it's your job to deliver a solution for a problem that person has. It isn't to be the most likeable person (although that's useful), it isn't to get a date (we're being professional, right?), and it isn't to be the funniest person they've ever met. It's to be a professional with a solution to their problem that's going to deliver them a prize, or win. Their problem will be solved, they will have peace of mind, they will find relief; whatever outcome the prize delivers.

The best salespeople match their solution to the customer's problem and communicate the value of the prize. End of story.

Listening

The old adage, 'Two ears, one mouth,' is true. As is another one: 'When you're talking you're only learning what you already know.' And may I also remind you of our wise owl, who has very very good hearing, and listens carefully to ensure he has heard the right sound, from the right animal before he acts. Listening is one of the most potent weapons a salesperson has. But it is a rare skill.

People respond positively to other people who listen well and then repeat what the speaker has said to reinforce that they have heard the message. If you do nothing more than be the best at understanding what someone tells you, at understanding their problem very clearly, I guarantee that you can be the best person on the planet at selling. Salespeople who listen and then relate their solution in the context of what they heard *are* the best salespeople.

Conversely, the worst salespeople are those who can't get out of their own way in their attempt to force their solution on the customer, even if that solution isn't a good one for the problem that's been identified.

If you listen to a prospect and then realise that your solution isn't for them, you should say so. People respect integrity, honesty and genuine help. They don't respect product floggers. And down the track, they may even refer you to someone who needs your product because they appreciated your honesty.

Identifying and handling objections

Many salespeople seem to think that the client's objections are an invitation to a knockdown drag-'em-out fight or argument. They're nothing of the sort. They're simply an indication from the customer that they haven't yet seen the value in the proposed solution.

If someone gets your value, believes it, and it solves their problem, they will buy it.

If your solution is no different to someone else's that's cheaper, they will buy that option.

This means that the whole process of handling objections comes down the five steps:

1. Listen to the objection
2. Understand the objection
3. Clarify the objection
4. Provide further evidence of your value in relation to the objection
5. Close the sale, or continue the conversation until you have done so

Will you make every sale? No. Because the reality is that your solution will not be the best solution for every prospect. If it is, it is. If it isn't, so be it. Move on. Don't get into an argument and try to sell someone on something that doesn't solve his or her problem. And don't be offended if they do object. Acknowledge it and handle it, or move on and let someone else solve their problem for them.

The close

You can read all the sales books you like, written by all the gurus on the planet, but a lot of these books offer methods to try and sell the unsellable; and to close every client, even those who don't want to buy, are not ready to buy, or who know the suggested solution isn't for them.

These books are for vacuum salespeople and used-car salespeople— the salespeople in any industry who don't understand or don't have a relevant differentiated benefit to offer. They are for product floggers (although I'm not saying that all vacuum salespeople and used-car salespeople are product floggers).

If a solution has true value, and the customer has reached the point where they see that value and agree with it, the close in a sale is nothing particularly dramatic. It's simply a point where the two parties agree to do business, and the salesperson has closed the deal.

It's also not an ending, as some salespeople would have you believe. The deal might be closed, but that's really just the beginning. For many companies, ninety per cent of the effort goes on delivering on the promises of value that the salesperson has made.

But even the salesperson's job doesn't end there. A good salesperson will now take full responsibility to ensure their customer gets the best value they've ever had in their life as a result of making the decision to buy from them.

How do they do this? Complete the following exercise and read on.

Exercise: Write down a list of three objections you've had from clients: too expensive, not big enough, too slow, whatever. Work out how a great salesperson would respond to these in the context of your business. How would they handle the objection and prove value?

Handing over to the organisation

When a sale is made, the salesperson is responsible for introducing the customer to the organisation. This will be covered in more depth a little later in the book, but for now we're looking at the basics of what a salesperson should communicate to the rest of the business about the new customer:

- Communicate the win to all other staff via the appropriate channel.
- Collate all the customers' details, including the order and their full contact details, which means processing invoices, etc.

- Organise for the customer to meet whoever will be looking after them: account manager, customer service, or production.
- For an appropriate period of time, continue to ensure that delivery is occurring and the customer is happy. This means checking in with both the customer and the client-service team.

Chapter 28
Advocating for the Customer

I've seen instances, and experienced them myself, where as soon as the deal is done, the salesperson drops the prospect like a ton of bricks on the doorstep of the business and are never heard from again. This is not good practice.

I recently purchased a new phone system for my office. I decided to go back to a past supplier, so I sent them an email and received a call from a helpful salesperson. I knew what I wanted and was already sold on using the company, so the process was pretty simple. I signed the deal sheet, and didn't hear from the salesperson for more than two weeks.

Also, I started to get emails from other parts of the business, with more forms that I didn't know were coming, including a third-party finance company I didn't know was involved. All of this would have been fine if the salesperson had taken the time to explain to me what was going to happen next. He could have said, 'Okay, the deal is done. Now I'm going to get Matt, our technical guy, to call you about installation, and Tammy, who's with our finance partner, to call about the paperwork.' The process would have been simple. I would have been informed.

But I got none of that, and although the sale is still proceeding it hasn't been without its frustrations and time-wasting moments for me. Why, for example, didn't the salesperson communicate all my details to the finance company so I didn't have to provide them all again?

A sale doesn't end with the sale; the salesperson is continually selling to the client the whole time they are making the purchase. This could take years, and every communication or lack of communication from the business is and always should be of interest to the salesperson that made the original sale. After all, the reputation of the business is reliant on the other parts of the team, so they should be interested in the business delivering on the promises the salesperson made.

Exercise: Write down five ways a salesperson can ensure that the rest of the business delivers on their promises in the first two weeks of a new client relationship. Make it applicable to your actual business.

Making the client an advocate of your business

I' I keep this section very simple. The only way a client will advocate for your business, or refer your business, is if they have been delivered great value. Not just fair value, not just good value, but *great* value.

Exercise: Write down five ways in which you demonstrate value to your customers. Write down what you think would be the difference between fair, good and great value in these five factors. For instance, fair value might be delivering at around about the time you said, good value would be delivering on time, great value would be delivering earlier than promised, along with a bonus, unexpected added-value item.

For example, fair value might be mowing the grass as you said. Good value would be sweeping the clippings off the paths. *Great* value would be doing the edges and watering the garden afterwards as a bonus.

Introducing clients to your organisation or team

One of the key functions to break down in a company is the introduction of a customer to the business once a sale is made. The salesperson is most definitely responsible for introducing the customer to the organisation in a seamless manner. In many cases, as far as the customer is concerned the salesperson *is* the organisation. In most cases the customer has never spoken with anyone else, and they might have developed a strong bond with the salesperson during the sales process.

For a salesperson to drop the customer like a hunk of meat at the front door without a proper handover and transition is very dangerous practice indeed.

Consider the following scenario. A salesperson makes a sale, then comes back to the office with the order form and drops it in an in-tray in admin or finance with no communication. The admin person is busy, doesn't notice the order form and so doesn't read it. They head off for the weekend without having handled it. The money is not processed. The customer doesn't get a call.

Come Monday, it's a busy start to the week. The admin person doesn't get to their in-tray until late Monday afternoon, and then decides to leave it until Tuesday. The problem is, the customer needs the item on Wednesday, and the turnaround time from order to delivery is tree days.

If the order had been processed on Friday, there would have been no problem. But now the order can't be delivered until the coming Friday. The customer is angry. Lost sale.

Extreme example? Yes, but I'll bet it's happened at least once this week, to at least one company somewhere on the planet.

Solution? In a business, you have to think of yourself as a station on a train network. Someone at the previous station puts a package on the train, sends it to you, and then you do something with that package and send it on to the next person.

In this situation, the marketing person sends a lead to the salesperson, who does their job and makes a sale. The salesperson then passes it onto the next person. Depending on the business, the next person could be in accounts and needs to set up a client account, process the order and get it into the system. Or it could be the office administrator. Or it could be you, wearing a different hat.

It doesn't matter who it is. What matters is that the salesperson helps coordinate a seamless transition to accounts, or the customer service person. Whoever it is, the customer should feel that they are being looked after, and is given a good explanation of what's going to happen next. For instance, 'We'll process your deposit, and then contact you with a delivery timeframe.' Or, 'Give me until tomorrow morning and I'll come back to you with a timeline for processing the policy you've purchased.'

Information is like a soothing balm on a burnt finger to a customer who wants to know the next steps, or when they can expect to receive what they have paid for.

Sales represent a link in the chain that results in a happy customer who values what they have purchased from you: a box, a drink, a dinner, a software system, an insurance policy, or a marketing plan. It doesn't matter what the product is, sales has to help transition.

The marketing and sales connection

Now let's look at the connection of sales into the organisation in the other direction. While the salesperson is making a sale and passing the customer onto the delivery contact, they are also receiving a lead from the marketing team. This integration is just as important because the sales team should be holding marketing to the same standard as described above. Marketing hands the lead to the sales team with information and details about what should happen next. What the prospect has enquired about would be a good start. Their phone number, email address and a scheduled time to call would be useful, too.

If the sales person doesn't get everything necessary with respect to the lead, they should send it back to marketing to get all the agreed information first.

Likewise, after speaking to twenty, fifty or a hundred prospects, the salesperson may well be knowledgeable about the needs and wants of the target audience. They will observe common objections; they will hear suggestions from customers on how to improve the product; they will hear war stories of poor service from the delivery contact or customer-service contact.

This should all be fed back to the marketing person, and the delivery person, to help them improve what they do.

All this means that a salesperson, like anyone else in the organisation, is responsible for their role, and being the best at it. They are also responsible for providing feedback to their colleagues to help those people do a better job. This does not mean pointing the finger; rather, it will help the whole organisation perform better.

Because the salesperson is often the first person the customer meets, and also very often the person who makes certain promises about quality, delivery, performance, and so on, they are a very important contact for the customer, and likewise they need to be an advocate for the customer in the organisation.

To the extent that they do this, they will find their sales process becoming easier in the future. Marketing will deliver better leads, and better-designed products and services. The service and delivery teams will do a better job of looking after the customer the salesperson has delivered.

Take-outs from Step 5

1. Who is your ideal client?
2. Make a list of people in your network who match this ideal and make some appointments.
3. What is your pitch? How are you going to sell your business to a prospect?
4. Write out the process/steps of sales to delivery of the product/service (then examine it from the customers viewpoint)

STEP 6
DELIVERING ON PROMISES

Chapter 29
Producing Your Product or Service

Here's an interesting fact for you about Owls – they are mostly monogamous and form long term bonds with their partners. They solidify their promises to mates with screeching displays and gifts of dead mice. Now I'm not suggesting you give dead mice to your clients, but delivering on promises and being faithful to your word is a great strategy in business. And most businesses become successful by forming long term bonds with clients, so if I may push the analogy a little bit further, promises and bonds and being true to your word have a big place in business. Delivery on promises is perhaps the most important activity in a business. We can consider strategy, managing people, and managing money and quality, but it's all for naught if the product or service is not actually delivered, the product or service for which your customers have sought out your business.

You've created a demand, made a sale, and now you have to deliver what has been paid for. And you have to ensure that the delivery is, at the very least, what was expected, if not more.

The media is littered with examples of companies who were good at promises, but failed to deliver. I'm sure if you've ever wasted half an hour of your life watching *A Current Affair* or similar programs you would have seen evidence of this. In this era of social media, it doesn't take long to find someone complaining about a business that didn't deliver what they promised.

I'm sure the majority of business owners know what their product or service is, and many have the technical expertise or passion to deliver it. After all, that's what they started their business for. But sometimes running the business can get in the way.

Scheduling, time and project management

Let's start with the topic of scheduling delivery. Some years ago I ran a survey in my marketing business for a large manufacturing business and found that among all the factors contributing to why customers dealt with this business or not was the organisation's ability to deliver the product in full, on time. The problem was that most of the staff thought the customers wanted the cheapest price. They didn't understand that they couldn't promise every client the first delivery every day just to keep them off their backs.

In the end, a pivot away from discounting and towards a focus on DIFOT (delivery in full on time) added significant profit, and customer loyalty increased this business's value markedly.

It may seem simple to consider delivering a product or service to one customer, but most businesses at some stage run into the problem of too much demand and not enough time. Whether it's a service business like a plumber fixing taps, or a product business delivering bricks to multiple locations, the problem of delivering will probably become a barrier at some stage.

No business can afford to resource for peak periods because it would mean having too many staff or machines during quieter periods. But there are some simple methods for coping with delivery that will work in any business

Estimated production

Every business should have a known range of time that it takes to produce their product or their service. For instance, at Silver & Wise we can estimate the average time it takes to develop a marketing plan, or a website, or to set up a social-media page. Many years ago I didn't have this knowledge, and I found it very unprofitable to let staff have as long as they wanted to do a project. I had no idea how long it should take, so I found doing a proposal for new work very difficult, too.

The way to develop these estimates is simple. Make the product or deliver the service, then make *several* of the products and deliver *several* of the services. Keep an accurate time of these 'pilots' and base your estimates on these averages.

If you don't go through the process of estimating projects or product builds, you will never be able to resource your business correctly, and almost certainly you will end up unprofitable or out of business.

Some years ago, we had to build a large number of template websites for a national client for their intermediary businesses. We made an initial estimate of $1000+gst for each site. The first website cost us $4000+gst to deliver. Ouch! With thirty-nine to go, I was looking down the barrel of a very big issue. We solved the problem by breaking down the process of building the sites and creating specific checklists. Then we set about making the process as efficient as possible, like doing multiple domain registrations at the same time. In the end, we were able to deliver the forty websites at slightly less than $1000 and made a small profit on the project.

And this gives brings us to the second delivery tool.

The checklist

Every single product build or service delivery in your business should have a checklist associated with it. In fact, every single *process* in your business should have a checklist associated with it.

If you had seen Henry Ford's production line at Ford in its first few weeks, I'm sure you would have seen chaos. People would have been running around like chooks with their heads cut off, picking up items multiple times, stopping the conveyor belts, and doing all sorts of inefficient exercises.

Look at your business for a moment. Go on. Take a look around.

How is your in-tray? Are there items in there that you've picked up multiple times, only to be interrupted and have to put them down again unhandled?

A checklist for a process has three main benefits:

1. It ensures everyone does that task the same way.
2. It speeds up production by reducing confusion about what to do next.
3. It ensures that you know where the process is, so if you have to put the item down you can come back to it and immediately pick up at the next step in the process.

And this brings us to the third item that will assist you with your delivery to clients.

Work-in-progress document

This document, along with an associated daily or weekly meeting is invaluable. A work-in-progress document (WIP) is a simple itemised sheet that details each project, the last and next actions, who is responsible, and when the product is due.

Every business that needs to coordinate multiple people delivering multiple products or services for multiple clients *must* have a WIP document, and meetings with customer services or account managers to review it regularly. How regularly will depend on the speed and complexity of the operation.

In our marketing business, we have a weekly work-in-progress report for the overall consulting practice, and also a work-in-progress report by customer that is sent to each customer each week, particularly those who have many marketing programs activated at any one time.

Our WIP document is a barometer, not only of the work in progress but also the resources required. It allows us to marshal resources around one person, or one client if that person is busy. It allows us to debug any projects that are stuck, for some reason, such as awaiting approval. And it allows us to track our productivity to see if there are items that have been on a WIP document for several weeks without moving along. We can see what is going on with that client.

A schedule board is a similar tool, and it's also valuable in coordinating delivery to clients. This is particularly useful in businesses where specific times have been promised for appointments or deliveries. With a glance at the schedule board, any staff member can know what's been promised by who and when, and prevents doubling up of appointments or deliveries. It also shows where each promised product is in the production line.

A scheduling board requires itemising the individual steps each product or service goes through in production. Of course, this can be done electronically, but it should also be on a screen, or printed out somewhere and displayed in the service or production area. That way, people can check it easily, without having to remember where things are or log in to find out.

To take another example from our business, we follow set production steps when we produce a brochure:

- Receive request from client to develop a brochure
- Write a brief on the brochure, giving all relevant information
- Get brief approved by client
- Give brief to designer to do initial design/layouts
- Get client approval of layouts, or refine until approval given
- Finalise artwork and get ready for print
- Send to printer
- Receive printed brochures
- Check for any errors and send to client
- File copies of electronic artwork and printed samples for future use

I'm sure if you took your product you could break it down into similar production steps.

In a research project many years ago, I interviewed a builder who was incredibly upset with our client, who had promised him a delivery of product for a roof he was building. The delivery was promised for seven-thirty am, and so the builder had organised his team of tradesmen to be at the site just before that time. The delivery did not arrive until ten-thirty. It had cost the builder three hours of labour for several people—a total cost of some several hundred dollars in lost production. Our client's local staff had promised several clients the same delivery time, and discounted their product as well. The builder told me he would have been willing to pay five or even ten percent extra for this product if delivery times had been honoured. This led to a pivot away from false promises and discounts to a slightly higher sale price and delivery promises that must be met.

Chapter 30
Delivering Products and Services

How would you define a product or service? This might seem a no-brainer, and most business owners would probably say they know what their product or service is. However, many businesses define 'fully delivered product' in a way that differs from their customer's expectations, and this is where they can get into trouble. In other words, in the customers' eyes they have not finished the job.

For example, let's say your product is insurance policies. Sounds simple, right? But an insurance company's definition of that product might be: 'Our product is an insurance policy that exactly matches what the customer wants and is told they are getting. The policy isn't complete or fully delivered until all the details are included in the policy, we have checked with the customer that the policy matches their needs, and we have filed the policy in our filing system with a date to follow up with the client in six months' time.'

If I had a dollar for every time I've received only part of a product or service I was promised, I would be a rich man. Let me give you some examples.

I recently ordered a phone system, which was delivered on time. Unfortunately the phone company had failed to brief the installers on my needs (as briefed to them) and I had to repeat all my instructions once again to the installers despite having already done so. Then the company had failed to order the Internet connection in a timely manner so I had to wait several days before that was put on, which was time critical for me.

Then I received the bill, and the charges were completely different to what had been promised in the original proposal. I went back to the company and wasted valuable time pointing out those differences so the invoice could be corrected. Needless to say, I was unimpressed.

Now imagine a different scenario, where the internal staff had a definition of their product: phones on, Internet on, customer-trained staff, invoice checked prior to sending, etc. Not only would I be satisfied, but I also wouldn't have wasted any of my time.

And now here's an example of the complete opposite of this, and what you should be looking to achieve with your clients. Recently, I needed to open a new bank account for our business. In any normal scenario, I'd have to go into my local branch and fill out all the forms, and then possibly go back when everything was ready. Not this time. I sent an email to my bank manager with the details, and she offered to drop the forms over to our house on the way home that night. She then took all the forms and then dropped back all our deposit books, cards and other information a couple of days later. Now I know I'm not a big customer, but we do have all our banking with this bank, and the manager knew I was in the middle of a large project for our major client – I didn't expect this service, and I was delighted with the extra attention and help from them.

My point is, if you define your product or service from the customer's viewpoint you can do a much better job more often, resulting in more satisfied customers who then become advocates.

Delivery on promises is incredibly important in today's ultra-competitive marketplace. If you don't do it, chances are someone who is more organised than you will take your customer.

Right person; right job

It goes without saying, but of course delivery on promises to customers requires you to have the right people in your delivery and customer-service areas, the right people making your products, and the right people delivering your service. So recruitment and training are also important factors in the delivery division of any business.

You can have undertrained staff in other internal areas of your business and get away with developing them over time, but putting incorrect, untrained or inefficient people in your delivery division is just asking for trouble.

A customer charter is another very useful tool in helping businesses deliver on promises. This is a statement of the company's promises and a great way to set customer expectations. The customer knows what to expect from the business upfront, and the staff also understand what is required to deliver a full and complete product.

Above and beyond

Doing a little bit extra may sound quirky, but you might be surprised to find that doing a little bit more than you promised and delighting your customer can have amazingly positive effects on your business. So, what is that little bit extra in your business?

I have seen numerous examples of this over the years, and have invested a lot of time and effort in helping our clients understand this for themselves. It doesn't have to be a big thing; customers will view something quite small in an amazingly positive light.

One example I've heard of, but haven't experienced personally, is the story of the most successful salesperson for Mercedes Benz in Moscow. This salesperson, let's call him Sergei, had the consistently highest sales every month for years. He also had the most significant return rate of loyal customers buying second, third and fourth vehicles from him over the years.

Was Sergei discounting his cars more than anyone else? Was he giving away more extras on each car? No. Sergei always delivered his cars with a bottle of high-quality vodka for the male customers, and a huge bunch of beautiful flowers for the female customers. And for everyone, he made sure the fuel tank was full on delivery.

Sergei paid for these things out of his own pocket. There wasn't a lot of expense involved—certainly not compared to the expensive cars—but his customers loved the little bit of extra attentiveness.

The other salespeople in the Mercedes Benz dealership were also delivering clean cars, with all the paperwork and everything else, but they didn't become famous among their clients like Sergei did. His extra gestures were done with genuine care and thankfulness for the clients' business.

A more recent, personal example is my local butcher. My family prefers to eat organic meat, which we can buy from a number of places, including the supermarket. But no one else except the local butcher throws in an extra sausage, or an extra hamburger with every sale. This small gesture has become quite famous in the area.

CHAPTER 30: DELIVERING PRODUCTS AND SERVICES

A final example is the tyre shop that donates money to the local community group for every sale. They don't make a big deal about it, but on each invoice there is a short note thanking the customer for their business, and also explaining that their purchase has contributed to a local project that is important in the area. This business doesn't give the customer something directly; instead, it points out that the *customer's* business has resulted in the donation, not theirs.

There are many ways to find that little bit extra and work to deliver it for your clients. See how it works for you. It's rare to see this today, so it might be the differentiator you need to compete more successfully in your market.

Some steps you can take to ensure you deliver on promises:

1. Make a list of every product or service that you deliver to customers in exchange for income/money.
2. Break down each of the steps or actions that are required to produce, prepare and/or deliver those products or services.
3. Next to each step, write down who or what role in the organisation takes care of that step, e.g. sales does a quote, accounts does an invoice, manufacturing makes the product, courier delivers it.
4. Make a list of every quote, order or product/service you currently have in production today/this week and the corresponding stage of production for each item.
5. Sit down with your team (or yourself, if you're a sole trader) and work out what the next step is on each of these existing quotes, orders or production items.
6. Get these next steps done and update the list. Focus on completely finishing each one on the list before moving to the next. For example, if you have two quotes and three products to make, finish a quote fully before moving onto another quote or product.

Don't jump from one to another unless you simply cannot do the next step yet.

7 Communicate to suppliers, staff or clients so they know what the situation is. This will minimise the need for clients or suppliers to call you, and also keep you functioning proactively. It may not be perfect to begin with, but if you follow these steps you'll move to being more proactive over time.

8 When you've delivered all current products, services or quotes, sit down and organise all the steps required to produce each different type of product/service in your business. Give this to each staff member who is involved in doing these steps. This is your production process.

CHAPTER 30: DELIVERING PRODUCTS AND SERVICES

Take-outs from Step 6

1. What tools can you use to schedule production of your product or service?
2. How are you going to make sure you can deliver on your promises?
3. What are three good questions you can ask clients to gauge whether you have delivered on your promises?

STEP 7
MANAGING QUALITY

Chapter 31
Quality Management

Owls know a thing or two about quality management. They are heavily reliant on their wings for flying, and they regularly preen their wings with an oil to keep them in top condition. And this goes further, because the preen oil can be converted into Vitamin D in sunlight, so the next time they preen they get a dose of vitamins too. Talk about keeping themselves in tiptop shape. In this chapter we discuss how your attention to quality can keep your business in tiptop shape too.

Over the years of running my business and in life, I've had many circumstances where a lack of quality in something I've bought or something I've delivered has been the difference between success, enjoyment and failure and disappointment.

Personally I've decided that I prefer to spend a little more to get a higher quality item that lasts, and I do all I can to deliver a high quality experience to my clients, doing more than expected.

The alternative of low quality, and products and services that don't do what they said is just too frustrating.

I've really only learned this through experience.

One thing that will ensure your business is sustainable and successful over the long term is the quality of your products and services. If you deliver what is promised, and ideally a little more than that, your business will be successful.

There are two parts to the marketing puzzle for a business: creating want, and delivering on promises. If a business promises something and doesn't deliver, that business is going to go out the back door pretty fast.

Failed promises are the source of much joy to journalists, newspapers and TV shows, so make sure you deliver on your promises. That's not so easy, you might say. And you'd be right, because this area of business is probably the least well handled across the economy, and probably the main reason behind a lot of business failures.

There are three key areas you will need to handle in quality management.'

Defining quality

The first area to deal with is defining quality as it relates to your business. Let's say, for example, that your business is making coffee cups. You could get the best coffee cup you've ever made and put that in a display box next to your production line as the standard you're looking for. You could tell your team that this coffee cup represents *quality*. This would be a simple demonstration of what quality is. Whenever the team makes a coffee cup, they can compare it to the quality cup and know instantly if the new item is also a quality cup.

Or you could be running a cabinetmaking or carpentry business. The client tells you they want every drawer in every cabinet to have tongue-and-groove joints. The client then comes along to inspect a cabinet you have made, and the drawers have are not tongue and groove. It would easy for them to tell you to replace the joints with tongue and groove. But without a written policy on that quality standard you wouldn't have known to do that. So there we have both the first and second elements of quality: set the standard, and then have a process in place where it's checked on a regular basis.

Quality is easy to define when you're dealing with a product, but not so easy when it comes to a service. You can, however, still define what a quality service is by the impact it makes on the business or the client.

If your job is to advise someone on how to set up their business structure, you could define a quality piece of advice by the documents, and the evidence that their business is in fact set up right: they have a business-name certificate, a bank-account structure, an ABN, tax-registration certificates, and so on.

If your service is courier deliveries, quality could be defined as making all deliveries on time, with all packages undamaged and all clients satisfied.

Checking quality

The second step to take in ensuring you have a good quality-management system in your business is to check quality. If you have a product company, this is a simple process:

- Schedule a random sample of product to be checked in inventory or on the production line.
- Survey a random selection of the last ten customers on quality.
- Step into the shoes of your customers and use the product or service yourself to test it. For example, get your nails done at one of your salons, eat your own food, or get your own pet minded at your pet-care centre.

- Employ someone to go mystery shopping and give you a report on quality of service of your front-of-house team, and the quality of the food being prepared by your chef.

If you have a service business, you could take some or all of the following actions:

- Randomly audit the files of your service team and check that everything that should be there is there. If you're working on your own, check over the last 20 transactions with clients and see where you could have improved your service.
- Survey customers of your company and ask if they are satisfied with the quality.
- Regularly review the forms and systems you use to ensure they are delivering a quality outcome. Are they clear? Are they being filled out properly? Could they be done better or differently?

For both product and service businesses, continue to spot check your quality. You can discover potential quality problems before they reach the customer. These checks don't have to be labour intensive or feel like you are holding you up, but they are important and will save you time and money in the long run.

In many businesses, checking quality isn't a habit. And in others, there are external agencies that are charged with checking compliance in your industry.

Keep in mind that if you don't check your quality, your client will do it for you. If they find it lacking, or if they don't get resolution, they'll buy from someone else. An external auditor will come in, like a health inspector. You'll be served with a notice, and put out of business for failure to comply.

CHAPTER 31: QUALITY MANAGEMENT

Quality is important in business. Of course, you must make sure your quality check is appropriate to your business's service or product. There's no point marking yourself down for not having hand-polished Huon pine wood on your tables if you're selling cheap laminated furniture. But even a cheap table would be expected to perform as a table by the customer, even if they only paid $50 for it.

Depending on the product or service you offer in your business, there may well be legislation, safety standards or other external influencers as checks on quality. It's important to abide by legislation, but simply meeting legislative standards doesn't always mean that you have satisfied the customer.

One morning I went to a local I for breakfast, and the business made this point for me. It was a nice place, with a funky design, and the prices were not at the cheap end. Fruit toast was, I think, $8 a serve. Which would have been fine if it had been baked on the premises, or was artisan-style bread, but what they served was lightly toasted supermarket fruit bread, and by that I mean *cheap* supermarket fruit bread; I saw the open packet as I walked past the kitchen on the way out.

Needless to say, the quality in this I didn't match the price and therefore I didn't value it at all. And I won't be going back.

Quality is a personal thing to your business, and it has to be pitched at a level that matches your market promise and customer expectations, while also allowing you to make a profit. If you were a violinmaker and you spent an extra fifty hours hand sanding and polishing the instrument you'd made but couldn't recover this in your price, it's clear that your business would suffer and not grow.

Not too long ago I was mentoring two friends who are in the marketing industry, providing similar, but distinct, services as myself. I had them do some work for me, and I saw on their invoice that their hourly rate was about half the usual rate for that type of service. The business owner nearly fell off his chair when I rang and asked him to double his invoice, and also counselled him to add a further twenty percent on top in any future invoices.

I knew from our discussions that this business had set some challenging goals for their business. But when I pointed out that they could never achieve those goals at their original hourly rate because they only had a limited amount of time, it became clear to them that they needed to reassess their rates. Not only were their rates well below the norm, but they were also below the quality the business was delivering—which was excellent.

Remember, your business is not a charity; profit means that you can continue to operate. But you still have to deliver value and quality or you won't survive.

Correcting quality

If you've set a quality standard, communicated it to everyone who has an impact on that standard and then you find that the quality standard is not being met in your regular checks, what do you do? Are you going to be reasonable about it? Perhaps you'll say: 'Oh, that's okay, maybe you didn't understand what I meant.'

Are you going to let an adviser get away with not filling in all the details that are required by legislation? No.

If a standard has been set, and everyone knows what that standard is, then you *must* correct it when you find it to be below requirements. So what can you do?

If you have a product business:

- Inform individuals of a gap in quality and explain what they should do about it.

- Retrain in the skills necessary to deliver quality.
- Check production lines and install new equipment if quality can't be met with existing resources.
- Go back to the suppliers of raw ingredients and remind them of quality standards, or switch suppliers if they can't meet what you need.
- Report on quality issues to authorities if health and safety concerns are not being not met or if a recall is required.

If you have a service business:

- Inform individuals of a gap in quality and explain what they should do about it.
- Retrain in the skills necessary to deliver quality.
- Set up new systems or policies to ensure that quality standards are met in the future.
- Make sure that staff understand the quality standard. It's important to find out what they missed and why. You could just need to review it more to ensure they get it.

Going back to our cabinetmaking example, the correction would be to replace the product with tongue and groove, and then have written instructions explaining how to stick to the quality standard in the future.

Once you become competent at each of the three areas of quality management, you may decide to implement higher level, more detailed systems, processes and so on. But focus on being proficient at the basics first. After all, you probably don't have unlimited time or resources.

Where does quality come in? It's probably better to ask the question: where *doesn't* quality come in? Quality is important in every single thing you say and do in a business. It isn't just about the quality of your product or service. It's what you promise in your marketing. It impacts the correctness of your invoices. It's important in how your product is packed for dispatch and much more.

Why is it important? There are a number of answers to this question, and they vary according to the product. It could be as simple as the product doing what it says it will do.

Let's say your business make coffee cups. What would happen if every time a customer put hot water in your coffee cups, the glaze came off, or the handle broke, or the liquid leaked out a crack in the bottom? (Don't laugh; I've bought coffee cups where these things actually happened.) In this case, the lack of quality would be obvious.

Quality could be a more serious issue. You might sell vaccines that hadn't been kept in cold storage continuously and so didn't protect against a disease. Or defibrillators with terminals that didn't conduct electricity and so couldn't be used to save a life. Or insurance policies that didn't actually cover the customer for what they wanted.

For the client, quality delivered equates to value received. And value received links to the current and future value of a business. So quality is not just a buzzword, it's something that is critical to get right in your business.

Take-outs from Step 7

1. Have you set your quality standard, describing it clearly so everyone involved knows what it is?
2. Write a quality checklist?
3. What steps will you take if quality standards are not met?

STEP 8
FACING THE FUTURE

Chapter 32
Adapt or Die

Owls are well known for their ability to adapt to different conditions that they come across. Many owls survive and prosper in urban conditions, and they will adapt their behaviour readily to ensure a ready supply of food and shelter wherever they find themselves. In business, having a similar ability will serve you well.

There's no doubt that the pace of change in most industries these days is much faster than ever before. The continued rise and use of technology has the potential to disrupt most, if not all, markets in coming decades. As mature individuals, we've all seen products and services become redundant, and this is happening faster than ever before. Not so long ago, we were listening to music on CDs and watching movies on DVDs; now we download or use streaming services. We once did our workouts with an iPod strapped to our arms; now we have smartphones.

As mature business owners, we must, now more than ever, keep an ear to the ground and an eye on the existing and potential competition. Not only do we want to avoid becoming redundant, but we also want to prosper in our ever-changing world.

In his book, *On the Origin of Species*, Charles Darwin wrote: 'It is not the most intellectual of the species that survives; it is not the strongest that survives; but the species that survives is the one that is able to adapt to and to adjust best to the changing environment in which it finds itself.' This quote has become the mantra of flexible, agile and adaptive organisations today.

Look for the opportunity to use technology to your advantage. In this chapter, we cover three important steps you can take to ensure that your business survives and prospers for as long as you need it to; namely: plan to adapt; pilot your ideas; roll out your ideas.

Plan to adapt

In this first step, there are some key concepts to be aware of. The first is to be aware. Many owners go through their business life blissfully unaware of what is going on in the market; they use the ostrich approach and stick their heads in the sand, hoping that trouble will pass them by.

Sailors used to talk about having 'a weather eye'. In a literal sense, it meant observing coming changes in the weather, but it's the metaphorical sense that we're more concerned with: keeping a constant and shrewd watchfulness and alertness.

How do you do this? There are several components:

1 Keep an eye on your main competitors in the market to check for any announcements of new products or services. For instance, a local competitor might launch a service that adds value to their products and increases their attractiveness to *your* clients, thereby increasing the likelihood they will defect from you.
2 You could set up a 'Google alert' for keywords related to your products and services. In this way, you'll be regularly informed of anything on the

internet that affects your market. It could be new research, or new entrants to the market. It could be new technology that you could take advantage of, or, at the very least, be aware of. You could also check news articles, announcements or industry websites for new trends and market launches.

3   In previous chapters we talked about regular customer surveys and how to conduct these. You definitely want to know how efficient you are at delivering what your customers need and want, and you also want assurance that you're still relevant to them. Regular surveys could highlight any deficiencies in your business, and pinpoint a heightened need for you to include innovation in your services. For example, clients might want to order or communicate online, and if you don't have a website, you risk losing clients to competitors who do. Websites provide quick and easy access to customer service, and if you don't have one I recommend you seriously consider remedying this.

4   Be aware of changing market attitudes. To use just one example, anyone in the taxi industry could have made better use of technology several years ago. Uber has invariably disrupted those who stuck with the old ways.

5   As part of your planning strategy, you could also have a mechanism or policy on how to respond to information. Do you have a process for dealing with new product- or service-development in your business? If so, does it include taking new ideas and assessing them against your existing business models? This needs to be monitored on a regular basis, and not just looked at every twelve months or so.

Pilot your ideas

Let's assume you've identified some new innovation, product or service that meets changing market demands. Do you rush right in, spend lots of money and possibly throw out the baby with the bath water? No.

Any new product or service needs to be tested in the marketplace before rollout. You need to iron out the kinks and get feedback so you can make refinements. You want to continue to make a good profit at the current volume and margin in your business.

The link between customer or market insights and new product development (NPD) needs to be clear and rigorous. NPD can't happen in isolation. It's means discovering something that will add value to your business, or your customers businesses, or, ideally, both. This discovery will come from a) your own experiences, b) listening to clients, c) watching the competition, e) obtaining data from formal customer-surveys, or f) all of these.

Before you make a change, make sure you're staying true to your overall client base and haven't drifted into another market. Most importantly, determine that it will add value and not cost.

All businesses need a method for piloting a new service or product with a select audience before rolling it out. Pilots have a few key elements:

1 Where? You may decide to pilot a new product in one store only, or one location.
2 Who? You'll probably select a small group of friendly clients for beta testing the product or service before you offer it to everyone. This can be a great way to engage with clients by giving them 'special advance' access at a reduced price in exchange for feedback on it.
3 What? You definitely don't want to involve all staff in a new product or service until it's been tested. If you run an existing business, you will want the current operation to continue without distraction so you don't lose ground. This means keeping pilots confined to one designated person, or doing it yourself so you don't interrupt current revenue and sources of income while the trial is underway. After all, it might not be successful, and then where would you be?

Roll out your ideas

After you've received rave reviews and proven you can make money from your new product or service, you're ready to roll it out. You still want to ensure that this new product or service fits with your existing business. Is it an additional service or product? Is it going to replace existing products or services over time? If you're a product a company, how much stock of the existing product do you have in the warehouse in the distribution channel, and will any have to be discarded or held in readiness to make way for the new product?

The rollout-and-measure phase is as critical as any stage that comes before it, so you still need to track all the steps involved in producing and delivering the product or service, as well as measure the impact it has on your business over a period of time.

Changes in products and services come with their own problems and opportunities, and you want to make sure there is more opportunity than problem in the mix. Will the supply be consistent? When you roll out, will the supply price be consistent with what you expect? What geographical issues are there? Is there a possible post-use issue for clients that you need to be aware of?

A final note on adapting

To reiterate, markets are changing faster than ever before. To continue to survive and prosper, the business owner needs to have their finger on the pulse, not only of the customer and the market, but also on who might come in and disrupt the status quo.

Business owners need to be prepared for an ever-evolving mix of products and services in their business to ensure long-term survival. No one wants to be stuck selling candles when light bulbs are invented.

Markets, customers and competitors are all complex beasts, but it's possible to survive as long as you know your value proposition, and how it will change for customers over time. If you can adapt as you go, you will not only survive but also prosper. If you don't or can't adapt, survival may not be something you can count on.

Chapter 33
What Does Success Look Like?

Having an idea in your mind of how you define success is important to you as a business owner. And the longer term the better. What is the end game? What do you expect to get out of your business in return for all your hard work? It's never just about money, but financial return is important.

I like to think of what this looks like on an annual basis, but also longer term than that. Having in my mind what success looks like allows me to compare how I am going on a day-to-day, week-to-week, month-to-month basis against my longer-term goals. I particularly like to fully encapsulate that success model in as many senses as possible. I'll give you an example.

Several years ago, when I was formulating our annual business plan, I wrote a couple of paragraphs describing what the business looked like when I closed my eyes. I described not only the revenue numbers, but also the office surrounds, what the staff were doing (active and productive), what sounds there were (phones ringing, happy banter), even down to envisaging a cafe in our office serving quality coffee and food to our staff (this had nothing to do with our business at the time).

A year later I was reading this business plan again when I suddenly realised that everything in my statement was actually occurring. The only thing missing was the cafe—but there was a high-quality cafe next door.

Engaging your senses, describing how you feel, setting financial targets, describing the sights and sounds of your business is a cool way to write a vision or ideal-environment statement for your business. A longer-term one might include you selling the business, or making enough revenue to not only pay off debts but also donate money to your favourite charity or whatever appeals to you personally.

Making sure you know what success looks like allows you to know when you are on track—and off it, too. What does success look like to you?

Chapter 34
What Is Your Exit Plan?

Personally I don't think owls consider the future, but they can obviously learn from the past and some owls do some amazing things, which just serve to emphasise their reputation for being smart, wise and experienced. Did you know that some owls use animal dung to improve the success of their hunt? The burrowing owl collects and arranges dung around it's burrow and then sits and waits for dung beetles to drop by for an easy meal.

So they learn from experience, and one area of experience that is important in business is that business owners should have an exit strategy planned out well before they need to action it.

This chapter discussed the concept of exit strategy.

I believe, this is even more important to the mature business owner like you. Because the start and end of your business ownership journey will most likely be closer together than the younger entrepreneur. You may only want to run your business for 5, 10 or 15 years. And a successful exit strategy can take between 4 and 8 years to execute.

A specific example of an exit strategy is succession planning, but in truth there are many varied exit strategies you could employ when you eventually want to cease operating the business yourself. Let's talk about those different exit strategies and how you can plan for them.

Planning ahead is the best way to handle these strategies. The future is often uncertain, and you don't know what's going to happen to you personally in the future. If you have a plan in place for all eventualities, at least you will have more control over the process.

Businesses cease operating for a variety of reasons, some of which are in the control of the owner and some of which are not. The ideal game plan is for the business owner to increase the options that are in their control, and reduce the options that are outside their control.

You may have heard of the four D's: death, divorce, disease and disinterest. Well, these do cover a bunch of reasons why a business ceases to operate, or needs to be wound up and closed, but there are other reasons that are external to the business owner's sphere of influence, such as increased competition, changes in technology, cheaper overseas products, changes in legislation, war and so forth.

For the moment, we'll leave the four D's for other experts to advise on. What we're interested in is the circumstances over which you can have some control.

Planned retirement

At the beginning of this book we talked about mature-age individuals being made redundant or wanting a change from their current corporate careers. For some mature-age people, this situation results in early, unplanned retirement because their employer has forcibly retired them and they can't find other work.

CHAPTER 34: WHAT IS YOUR EXIT PLAN?

If you have started a business now or are about to, and you plan to retire on your own terms a few years down the track, now is the time to think about this plan.

When you do retire, what do you want to do with the business? Are you happy to simply run it until that day and then close the doors? Or would you like to sell it to someone?

Would you like to step back from the day-to-day, but keep a shareholding in the business and let someone else run it? Or do you not care as long as you make enough income now and during the running of the business?

Whatever you decide, it is smart to have some plans in place now to ensure that the outcome you want is within your control.

I did some work with a real-estate agency a few years back, in which the owners of the business had a smart, long-term plan to exit. They identified senior staff in their business, and had a program that offered small shareholdings of the business, each year, to those staff at the current market value of the business. The small parcels were easily within the reach of the staff to purchase, and allowed a staged exit of shareholding by the owners at fair market value. It also meant that when they retired they wouldn't have a huge shareholding to sell off, and their natural successors were already invested in the business.

If, on the other hand, you thinking about selling your business in the future, remember that this process can take up to five or six years from the time you decide to do so. Most buyers will want to base their purchase on three or four years' worth of financial results, and you as the owner will want to maximise the sale price when you do exit.

This could take you a few years to achieve, so you may want long-term plans in place to ensure that revenue and profit is growing at the time the sale is made.

The value of a business can be based on more than just revenue and profit. A buyer might pay more if your database is up to date, if you have long-term contracts to supply your product to customers, and if your business is well organised, with excellent systems and processes and the value of goodwill. All of this takes time to put into place.

If you want to keep a smaller shareholding and have someone else run the business, how long will it take to find that person and then, over time, hand over the day-to-day operations of the business?

What roles will you play in the future? Will you be a silent shareholder, or the annoying partner who insists on the new person running it just like you did? If so, who is going to put up with you?

All these things need to be taken into account and actioned over time, and that takes organisation. Put this against the backdrop of a glut in the supply of businesses for sale as baby boomers retire, without enough demand from gen X, Y or millennials to buy those businesses, and you can see that good planning will be required to make sure you achieve your own personal exit goals.

Don't leave it all to chance.

Exit on your own terms

Throughout this book, I have focused a lot on making assumptions, and ensuring that you keep connected to customers to know what they need and want. This strategy is also important when considering a business exit. You can't make the assumption that someone will be there to buy your business when you want to sell. You also can't make any assumptions about your health, or how markets will perform, or how good your competitors will be in the future.

But what you can do is continue to take stock of the situation, be aware of market dynamics, and put in place as much planning and strategy as you can to minimise an exit on someone else's terms. Plan the exit from your business as well as you planned the entry and you'll be in better shape than most business owners.

You may be already up and running with your business. You may still be thinking about the opportunities ahead and what type of business you'll operate. You may have decided that running a business isn't right for you now. Either way, it's up to you.

If you do decide to run a business, I want you to know that I believe you can do it. And I believe that the decision is important not only for you, but also for your whole community and the economy as a whole.

We need people like you—mature-age people with wisdom and experience—to be productive in our society, for their own sakes, and also for their communities. After all, it's productivity that drives the economy and makes available resources for all of us to achieve our personal and social goals.

Productivity drives happiness, revenue, profit, income, taxes, philanthropy and social betterment.

Without people like you being productive, we are worse off. Long live Experience, thank you, and good luck.

Take-outs for Step 8

1. Before you start your business, can you think of some trends that could impact your products and services, so you can adapt to them along the way?
2. What is your exit strategy? Write down some thoughts about this.
3. Write down your top three things that you could do this week to start your business. Good luck!

About Silver & Wise

I trust that you have enjoyed this book, and that it helps you get a handle on the key skills you'll need as a business owner. Clearly, a book of this nature cannot give comprehensively detailed coverage of every skill area, and my recommendation is to take it as the basic framework for starting a business. After reading it, you can add more details from further learning, or from finding expert advisors to help you in each key skill area.

Should you choose, you might consider enrolling in our business ownership course at Silver & Wise, where you'll not only learn more, but you will also connect up with like-minded entrepreneurs you can cooperate, work or network with through our Silver & Wise Alumni Program.

In our alumni program, we aim to measure the success of business owners who have joined our advisory team, and those who have read our books and completed our courses. We are interested in seeing the measurable impact that successful and productive mature people can make on the economy. We invite you to visit our website and give us a personal report on your progress in running a business. Tell us how you're doing, whether you're profitable, employing people, and meeting your financial goals.

Collectively, if we track your success we'll know what we've achieved together. Join our alumni as an interested observer, contributor, course participant, advisor, or productive and successful business owner.

Our mission

Silver & Wise was created with a single mission: to change the lives of mature individuals through business ownership. We've researched in depth over the last two years and found that in Australia we are wasting the experience and wisdom of those in the forty-plus age group. Many people are being made redundant. The numbers of people who are willing to work are growing exponentially, and on average they take twice as long to find a job. Many people—27 per cent, in fact—report being on the receiving end of age-related discrimination, and a third of these people give up looking for work believing they are 'past it' and unemployable.

We are not alone in looking at the problem of finding mature-age people work, but we have additional expertise in running businesses, and have chosen, as our part of the overall social issue, to help those mature individuals who have decided to start their first business at forty or over.

Mature-age business-ownership program

Silver & Wise is offering a mature-age business-ownership program for those individuals who want to start their own business but don't know quite how to go about it, or feel they have some skills gaps in certain areas of running a business.

We have a range of introductory and more advanced courses, workshops and coaching programs available to individuals who are on the journey to starting their own business.

We want to hear from you. Send us a note via our website: www.silverandwise.org.au.

Mature-age advisory network

One of our models for helping mature-age people start a business is to focus on something we know very well: running a strategic consultancy.

With seventeen years of business ownership behind us, and an enormous amount of intellectual property on successful and proven strategic planning and marketing, we've focused on creating the first-ever national network of mature, strategic marketing advisors.

They will run their own businesses under our umbrella, with head office support to generate business opportunities, and develop products and services that will help them advise small-to-medium-sized businesses, and their owners.

In five years, we plan to have up to twenty-five individuals running their own businesses within our network. It is Australia's first mature, strategic advisory network.

About the Author

In his Blue Frog Marketing business, Hunter Leonard researched over ten thousand business owners in the small-to-medium enterprise (SME) space, including one of the largest marketing benchmark ever created in Australia. Hunter understands that most business owners don't have general-management skills for running their business, coming, as they often do, from a technical-specialist side of the field or market of their business. No one has taught them how to be a general manager, or a business owner, and they usually have to cobble together a method of running their business from their experiences of running into issues and barriers.

In creating the Silver & Wise Business Ownership Program, Hunter has designed a comprehensive, practical learning experience that results in the participants being both competent and confident in the key skills they need to be a successful business owner.

Outside of work, Hunter is a keen musician, cook, and photographer, and loves getting out into country Australia or the bush away from the computer and the office.

He is driven, passionate, and wants to make a difference to individuals, communities, and the economy as a whole. That is why Silver & Wise was created.

www.ingramcontent.com/pod-product-compliance
Lightning Source LLC
Chambersburg PA
CBHW070355240426
43671CB00013BA/2506